Course Design
A Visual and Modular Approach

Course Design
A Visual and Modular Approach

Jacques Lanarès
Marc Laperrouza
Emmanuel Sylvestre

Graphic design and illustrations
by **Julian Bader**

Forewords

This book is the link we've been missing!

A link, unaffiliated with any one discipline, between the learning sciences and the practical development of a course.

A link, both daring and stimulating, between an intuitive perception and an explicit understanding of what it is to teach.

A link, both interactive and fun, between one's own experiences and aspirations in the world of teaching and a coherent teaching scenario.

Going through the step-by-step elements of constructing a teaching course is like analyzing a work of art: the mystery of its success is never completely resolved. But this only makes us marvel at it all the more and feel motivated in our own creative process.

Give it a try and have fun!

Prof. Giorgio Zanetti
Vice-Rector for Education
University of Lausanne (UNIL)

All new courses start off with an idea. For many of us, this first step is the easiest, but for a new class, workshop, or any other teaching activity to be successful, we need more than just an idea. We need a clear vision of the desired outcome and the necessary skills to achieve it. And that is precisely where this book comes into play, by outlining the path we should take. From design to professional development, it tells us all we need to know about teaching.

This is a fantastic guide for those who love to teach!

Prof. Béla Kapossy
Former Dean and Director
of the College of Humanities
Swiss Federal Institute of Technology
in Lausanne (EPFL)

Preface to the English edition

Behind this book lie three colleagues who have different academic profiles and backgrounds but who are driven by the same passion for teaching and learning. Three colleagues who have been confronted, each in varying ways, with the multiple challenges that they pose, from the organization of learning activities to course design.

But the book also emerged out of an observation: that among university-level books on teaching and learning there is no broad-based, multipurpose, and intuitive tool that can be applied to varied teaching domains. This book aims to fill that gap. Created to suit experienced teachers, those beginning their career, and professional training instructors alike, it takes a practical, visual, and modular approach.

This book is designed for those instructors who like to reflect on their teaching approaches and want to broaden their field of vision, take a global approach to their teaching, and explore issues of pedagogy without feeling they need a PhD in learning sciences.

It provides a three-step approach that guides readers through a process that will allow them to define their understanding of the teaching and learning process, build or revise a course, and develop their teaching skills.

Some of the terms used in the French edition of this book do not have exactly the same meaning in an English-speaking context, in particular because the theoretical frameworks are different. In several cases, we have therefore had to make a decision on which terms to use, and we hope we have correctly translated the concepts presented in the French edition.

A Three-step Approach

Envision

Define your teaching philosophy to clarify your role

Design

Build or revise your course and develop teaching scenarios

Develop

Take a step back from your teaching practice to gain perspective and bring out its value

Clarifying your teaching intentions helps you make choices when developing your course, making it easier to communicate your expectations to the students.

Designing a learning experience requires you to successfully organize four basic elements: content, learning outcomes, the teaching and learning strategy, and the assessment strategy, while taking the context into account.

Analyzing your teaching experiences allows you to continue developing your professional skills and improve your teaching methods.

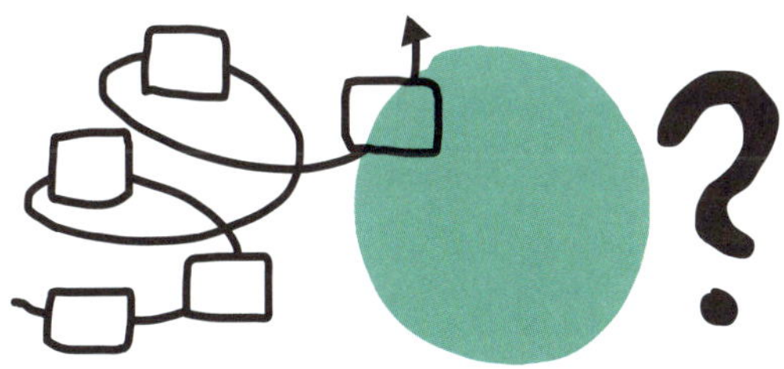

The Aim of the Book

Our Intentions

The aim of this book is to help its readers develop a new course or analyze an existing one, while respecting the principles of constructive alignment. To facilitate this alignment, we have created a canvas that forms a guiding framework throughout the book and that will be described in the following pages.

The approach we propose is the result of a long process of experimentation and refinement. Although the book draws on a solid theoretical foundation of learning sciences, psychology, and sociology, these theories are not presented in detail; at the end you will nonetheless find a list of titles to further explore certain theoretical aspects.

The various steps in the approach will allow you to clarify your teaching intentions (Envision), develop a coherent learning experience (Design), and continue to improve your teaching skills (Develop).

This book takes into account three current priorities in higher education:

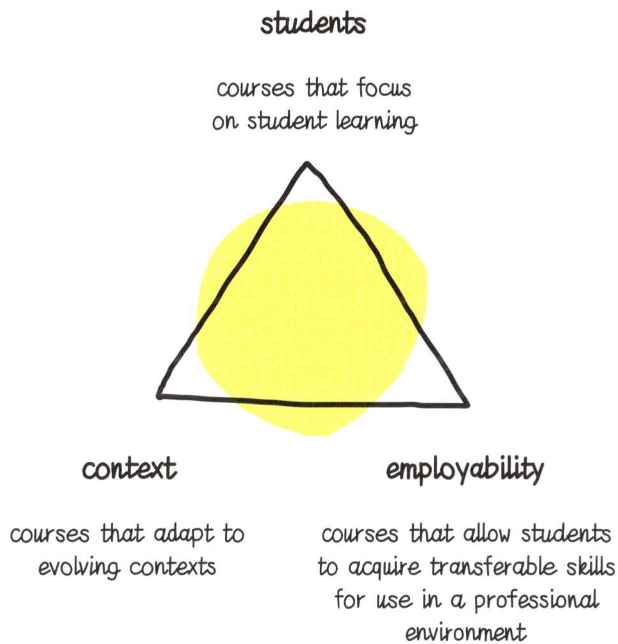

Our Philosophy

Practical

This book has been designed above all to be a practical tool. It draws on many years' experience in running workshops for instructors, and contains suggested activities to accompany you while you think about and design a student-centered learning experience.

Visual

Because we wanted the book to be accessible and appealing, we decided not to adopt the traditional style of an academic textbook. We have instead gone for a more visual presentation that encourages you to take concrete steps, with text reduced to a minimum and a particular focus on diagrams.

Modular

Depending on your needs, you can dip in and out of the book to find the right tools; you can apply our proposed methods to an existing course or to one you are in the process of developing, you can get straight to the point by aligning the intended learning outcomes with your teaching and assessment strategies, or you can take a more comprehensive approach by first understanding your own vision for teaching and learning.

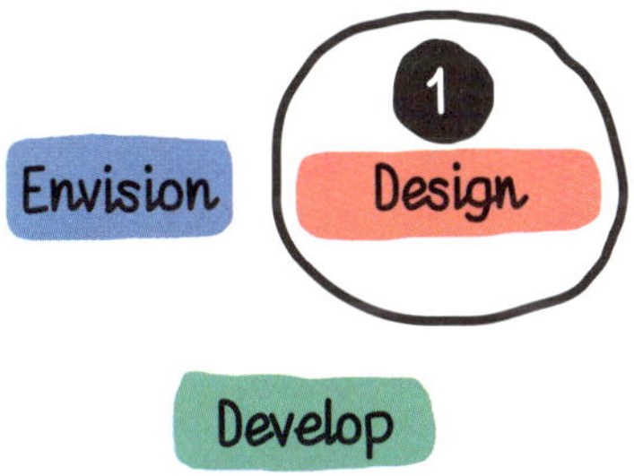

Design
a learning experience

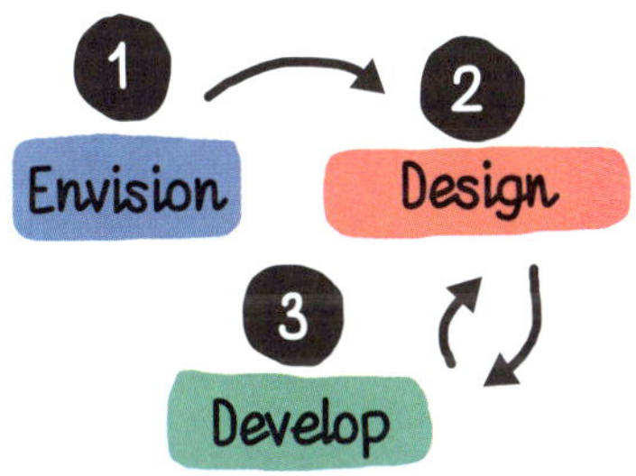

Shift from intuition
to intention

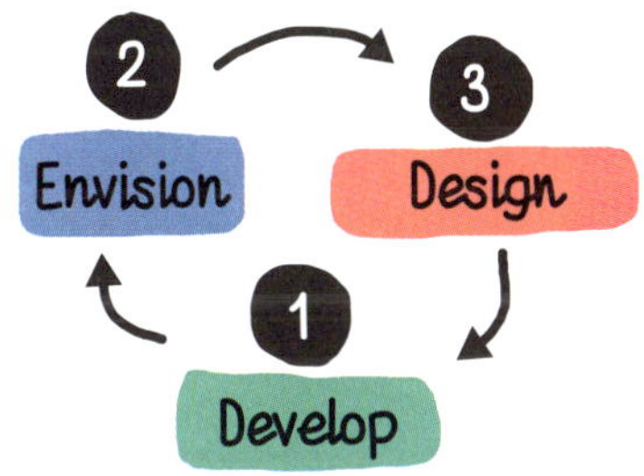

Gain perspective on your
current teaching approach!

Versatile

This book draws on our combined experience and, in particular, on the training workshops held at the Teaching Support Center at the University of Lausanne (CSE). The philosophy underlying our approach is that there is not one single, correct way to teach and/or train. There is no magical blueprint to follow. However, we do believe there is a set of key questions you should ask yourself when designing or revising a course or other learning activity. To each of these questions there is a range of possible answers, which vary depending on the instructor, the students, and the broader learning context.

As such, this book is intended to be non-prescriptive and non-normative. So rather than outlining a method that must be strictly adhered to, it instead poses questions to guide your thought process around the design or revision of your course. It focuses on the instructor, while at the same time incorporating key issues around students and their learning processes, as well as including elements that will allow you to make coherent choices about the design and implementation of your course.

Tools to Help Guide Your Thinking

As this book has been developed with practicality in mind, we have provided you with several different tools—the result of a long process of experimentation and refinement in various contexts. They can be applied to any teaching or training situation, and you can personalize or modify them depending on how you intend to use them.

Questions to Support Your Thinking

These provide the starting point for your process of reflection and are designed to make you become aware of your choices and then fully express them.

The Canvas

The canvas is the book's main tool, providing a framework for the process of designing or revising a course.

Examples to Illustrate the Key Concepts

In this book we have tried to avoid "tips and tricks" and instead focus on general principles, with the aim being to help you implement these principles within the context of your course. To help you draw connections between general concepts (necessary when dealing with a wide range of applications) and your personal context, we have included examples from a sample course on research methodology. This sample course runs throughout the book and gives a more concrete idea of the concepts and tools we present. It can be identified by the magnifying glass symbol with the letters "RM." More generic examples will sometimes be used and will be identified by the symbol without the letters.

Generic example:

Sample course Research methodology:

References to Extend your Knowledge

We wanted the book to flow smoothly so have chosen not to insert bibliographic references into the text. These references can instead be found at the end. They are numbered and can be identified by the below symbol.

Activities to Help You Get Started

This book has not been developed to simply increase your knowledge, it is also a tool to help you get started. That is why you'll get the most out of it if you use it to design or revise one of your own courses. By "course" we mean any learning activity ranging from a semester course to a three-day workshop, a 3-hour lab or a 45-minute lecture.

We encourage you to use this book alongside an actual course so you can put the suggestions into practice as you go.

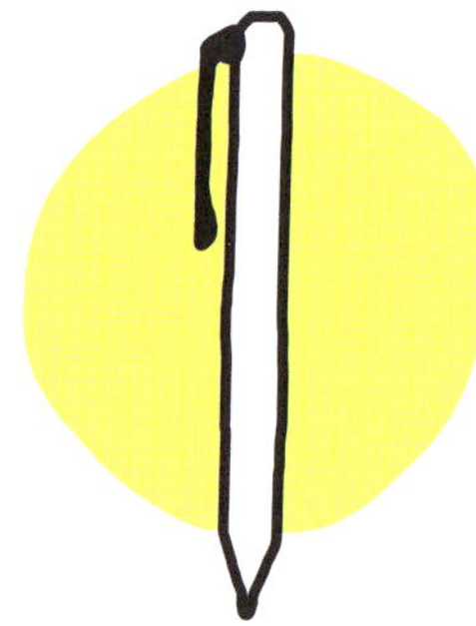

To do this, it would be useful if you gathered some equipment: teaching plans, descriptions and books related to your course, as well as sticky notes, a pen or pencil, etc.

Print out the canvas and complete it as you go through the book.

The above symbol lets you know it's time to do an activity.

Some steps may be more difficult than others (which is completely normal). You will find examples that give details about teaching and learning activities or assessment methods. In addition, the "Research methodology" example provides you with an illustration for each step.

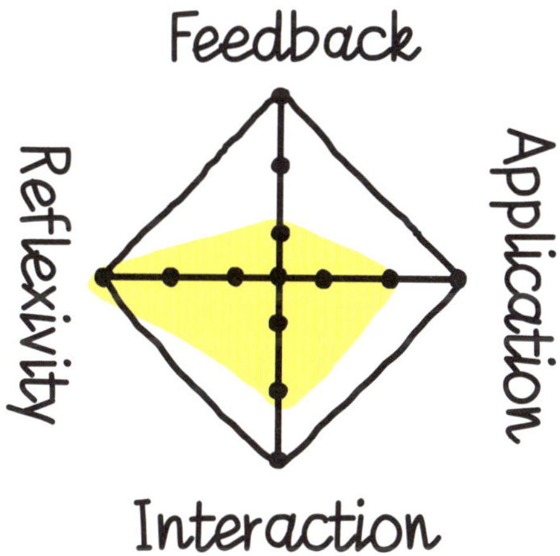

By following our approach from start to finish, you will end up with a complete course (or teaching scenario) that includes content, intended learning outcomes, a teaching and learning strategy, an assessment strategy, a syllabus, and a detailed roadmap for teaching.

Now, let's get started!

Envision

This section will allow you to fully explore and express your view of teaching and learning. This is often implicit and can unconsciously determine your teaching choices. Gaining awareness of your underlying views and expectations will enable you to clarify your priorities and express your choices. The following pages will help you through this thought process.

From Understanding Your Teaching Approach to Defining Your Teaching Philosophy

Instructors of all kinds often have implicit views of what it is to teach and learn. By clearly expressing your priorities, you will be able to justify your choices when designing a course, communicate these choices to students, and formulate a teaching philosophy. To help you become aware of your own implicit ideas and articulate your teaching philosophy, we have provided you with three activities: the first allows you to understand which of the traditional learning approaches you most resonate with, the second enables to you explore your own experiences, and the third will help you bring these aspects together into an expression of your teaching philosophy.

How You Relate to Different Teaching Approaches

The objects on the next page are above all designed to prompt your implicit understanding of teaching. There is no right or wrong answer! You can combine several objects or even choose one that isn't featured but that better reflects your sense of what teaching involves.

What is important is to use this object and the values it conveys for you as a launching pad to identify your teaching priorities—what is the main idea you associate with this object? As an example, people who choose the brick might talk about the idea of construction. Those who identify with the watering can often explain the idea of student potential that the teacher must nurture by providing the right "food."

Once you have this initial idea, the next step is to determine your priorities for teaching and learning. For example, those who identify with the idea of construction often describe a progression from simple to complex in which links back to the previous elements are developed. Those who connect with the idea of the watering can often speak about paying attention to student needs and the importance of creating the right learning environment.

Which object best conveys your idea of what teaching is about?

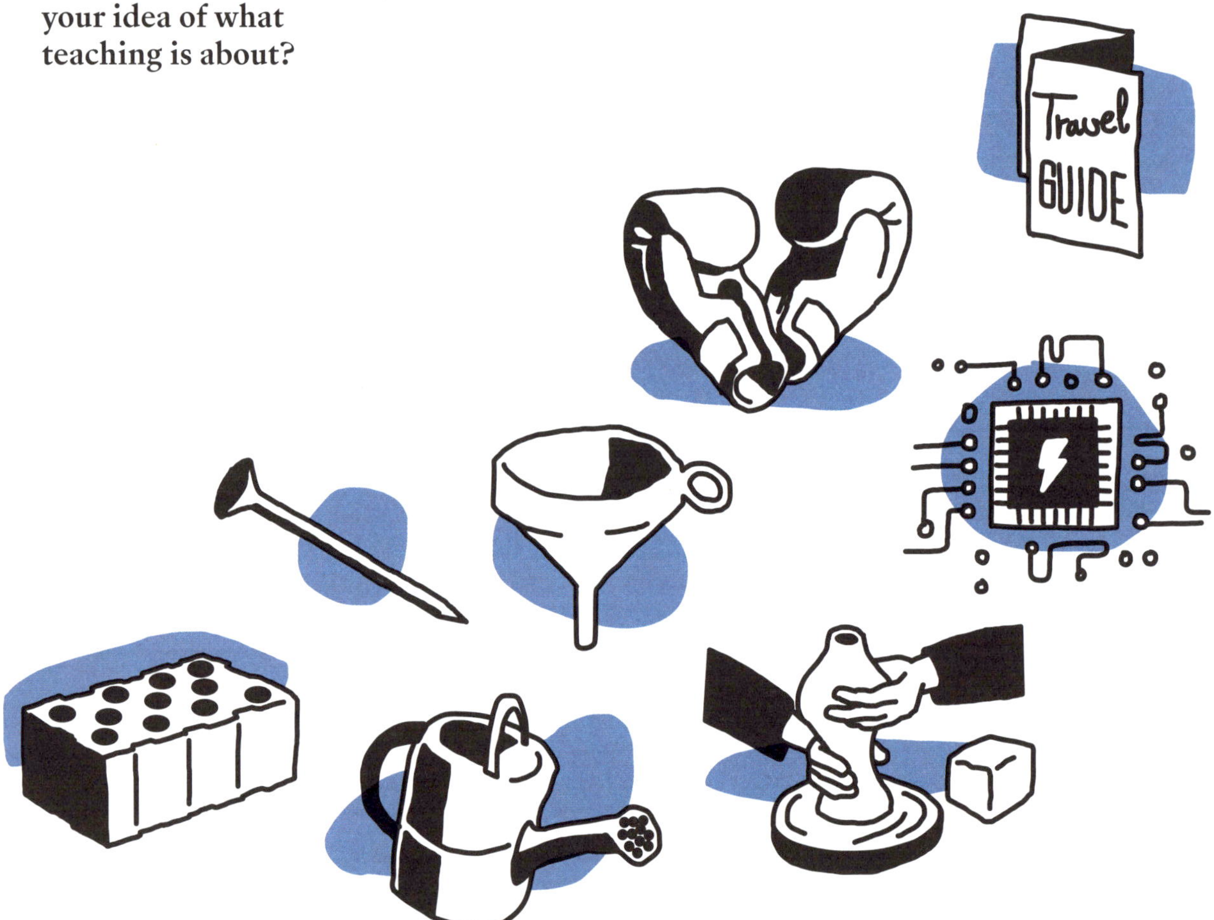

How does this object best convey your idea of what teaching is about?

The watering can illustrates two aspects that I care about:

1. Knowledge for the greatest possible number (compared to a tap);
2. Watering seeds in the hope of seeing plants grow.

Based on this idea, what do you focus on when teaching?

I see my role as being one of facilitating, embracing all points of view, and making sure that everyone reaches a minimum standard.

What are your expectations around the learning process and behavior of your students?

I expect my students to be prepared for each class and to actively participate in classroom discussion.

To start you off on the thinking process, we have selected different types of objects, which can be associated with a specific learning approach. A more detailed description of some of these can be found later in the book. Our intention here is to provide you with concrete ideas that will encourage you to think about your priorities.

Object	Teaching approach	Necessary conditions for the approach to work
Microchip 	This approach places special emphasis on information processing (illustrated by the microchip). It is in line with the cognitivist perspective.	Well-structured content Information in chunks, rhythm Allow the multiple coding of information (visual/aural, images/words, etc.) Encourage student appropriation of the content Regular repetition Put concepts into practice
Brick 	The brick conveys the idea that knowledge is built on previous elements. As such it can be associated with the constructivist approach.	Focus on connections • Connect to prior knowledge • Relationships between themes, concepts, lessons • Connect to other situations • Promote reflexivity, awareness
Modeling clay 	The idea behind this approach is that we learn by observing good practice (for instance, mentoring or surgical training).	Focus on important aspects and stages of a process, break the process down Multiple opportunities for practice with feedback Organize a learning process that aims for student autonomy (from simple to complex)
Boxing gloves 	The gloves illustrate the idea that interaction and contrasting points of view are necessary for developing understanding. The gloves can be linked with social constructivism.	Interactions • With students • Between students Contrasting points of view, critical thinking

Object	Teaching approach	Necessary conditions for the approach to work
Nail/hammer 	Hammering in a nail underlines the role of repetition, which alongside feedback is a major factor in learning. It is at the heart of behaviorism.	Organization • Clear objectives • Clear progression of steps Repetition Assessment/Feedback
Funnel 	The funnel illustrates the point of view that says that in a learning process, the instructor transmits knowledge to the student.	High-quality presentation • Clear explanations and coherent structure • Use of images, examples • Range of tools, multiple formats • Emotional component • Several ways of presenting High-quality content • Topicality • Relevance • Selection
Group travel guide 	This approach focuses on the role of the instructor as a facilitator, guiding the learning process based on the intended learning outcomes.	Respond to individual needs Acquisition of methods Socratic methods Assign projects to students
Watering can 	The watering can illustrates the notion that each human being has the potential for development and that the instructor must create the conditions for this to occur. It is related to a humanist approach.	Identify prior knowledge and adjust lessons accordingly Create an atmosphere of trust Use a variety of approaches and strategies Allow room for individual preferences and choices

Engagement and Motivation

Motivation is a key aspect of the learning process, and if you have a general understanding of how it works, it is easier to account for it when preparing learning situations for your students. It is not a question of studying the many motivation models that exist in the scientific literature, but rather of ensuring you have a broad understanding, enabling you to analyze the situations proposed in this book. Motivation cannot be directly observed or assessed, but it is visible through behaviors such as persistence, cognitive engagement, and participation.

Motivation effectively results from an individual process and cannot be "injected" into learners, contrary to the common belief that says: "You must motivate your students!" It cannot be stored up and used at a given moment. Motivation only exists as an objective—learning Mandarin, for example—or an activity—such as participating in a debate on the pros and cons of a certain method of analysis. As such, we are always motivated (or not) by something specific. In a nutshell, various studies on motivation can be summarized with the simple equation: $M = E \times V$, which says that motivation (M) depends both on a student's perceived self-efficacy in achieving an objective or completing an activity (E) and the value attributed to the result (V). As the equation suggests, if one of the two factors is low, motivation drops. For example, if I am interested in participating in a debate on the pros and cons of a certain method of analysis, but I don't feel I have the necessary skills to contribute, my motivation is almost certain to be low. Similarly, if I feel I have the skills to learn Mandarin, but I don't see the point, my motivation will again be very low.

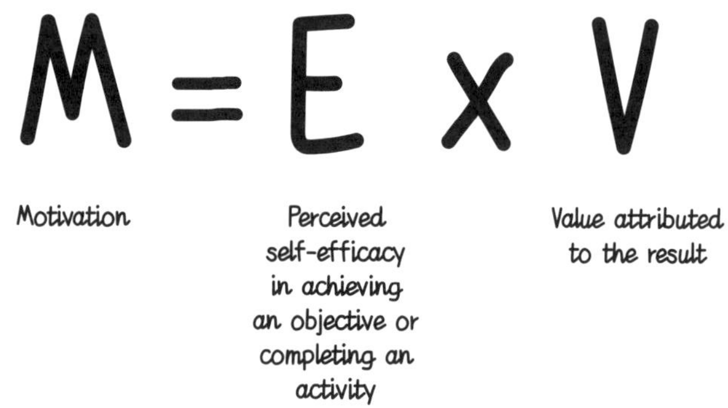

22

When designing and implementing a course, it is essential to create conditions that encourage students' perception of self-efficacy on one hand and that relate to their values and priorities on the other hand. Even though we cannot directly motivate students, we can create favorable conditions and increase the likelihood that they will become motivated.

There are several different ways that you can generate perception of self-efficacy: make connections with what the students already know (personal experiences, other classes, metaphors, examples from real life); ask them to summarize a lesson so they can see what they have already understood and retained; and encourage them to become aware of the various strategies they use and identify those that work. Furthermore, highlighting the connection a specific course or activity has with the intended learning outcomes (ILOs), as well as pointing out the personal, social, and professional repercussions of completing it, while clearly explaining the positive outcomes of their engagement can also encourage students to value a course or activity more highly.

Remember that a teacher's own motivation is extremely contagious!

Analyzing Your Own Learning Experiences

To continue the thought process around your teaching approach and expand on it, we have included some additional questions.

Note down which teaching priorities have emerged out of your personal experiences.

How do I best learn?

If I think back to the teachers I learned the most from, what did they do that was so successful?

Which of these personal experiences have I carried over into my work?

How do I best learn?

While I was studying, my strategy was to read textbooks and documents, underline what I understood to be key points, and make summaries of these to help me prepare for exams. I made sure I attended every class, even though I didn't participate much. Just before exams, I practiced some of the exercises we had been provided with during the semester. My approach has changed regarding one point in particular: during training courses, I try to come prepared and participate more.

If I think back to the teachers I learned the most from, what did they do that was so successful?

Some teachers made the subject matter particularly interesting, which motivated me to learn because:

1. The teacher managed to create a connection with the audience through a kind of empathy and/or the time taken to reply to questions outside of teaching hours.

2. The teacher made sure the classes were well structured and often repeated key examples. I remember one teacher, who over 4 semesters repeatedly used the example of a cup of tea in an alpine restaurant when talking about contract law.

3. The teacher gave us a practical project that made sense, or sometimes even let us choose our own projects.

Which of these personal experiences have I carried over into my work?

A bit of everything... but not necessarily all the time, or even in the same way! I believe that creating a connection with students is particularly important, as is ensuring that students find meaning in their learning journey.

The Students Are Not Your Clones!

The “massification” of higher education has increased the heterogeneity of student audiences. In addition, human diversity also generates individual preferences. There is a wide body of literature devoted to learning styles, which has attempted to classify students depending on their intellectual preferences or affinities.

When we teach, it’s normal to try and reproduce the conditions within which we learned best. But for this approach to be effective, the students need to behave as we did, which as the years go by is less and less the case... Only 5% of all first-year students go on to pursue an academic career. Their motivations, their approach to studying and intellectual pursuits, their affinity for abstract thinking, and their enjoyment of reading are some of the ways in which they may differ.

As these preferences can change over time, teachers should not pigeon-hole students. The two key words that emerge from this are decentering and diversity.

Meta-analyses carried out on this data do not result in clear-cut profiles, but do emphasize the importance of certain variables such as the kind of material (visual, aural, written, images), teaching approach (experimental, conceptualization, etc.), learning approach (surface, deep), relationship to authority and knowledge (level of epistemic development, generation XYZ), and a student's affinity for working in a group or preference for self-study. This is not an exhaustive list.

Formulating Your Teaching Philosophy

The thinking you have done about teaching up until now can be summarized by your "Teaching Philosophy." This philosophy can be defined in various ways, but essentially it conveys your beliefs and theories about teaching and the priorities that result from these, as well as your expectations of students.

- What do you believe is the end purpose of higher education?
- What are your priorities as a teacher?
- How would you describe your role as a teacher?
- How would you describe the role of the students? What do you expect from them?

Based on your answers, what can you say about:

- The importance of interactions in the learning process?
- The importance given to practical elements (examples, exercises, projects, etc.)?
- The influence of different experiences (visual/aural, physical experience, images/words, etc.)?
- The importance you give to the students' prior knowledge?
- The way in which your teaching is structured?

This analysis can help you identify your teaching priorities. Once you have finished designing your course, it would be useful to ensure that the choices you have made reflect your vision.

Obviously there is no wrong way to formulate your teaching philosophy, however, it is important that it reflects your vision and priorities, and that students and your colleagues can easily understand it.

One simple way to begin writing it down is to refer to the following model, which you can complete.

My main objective as a teacher is... To achieve this, I... In turn, I expect the students to...

My main objective as a teacher is to help my students in their learning journey. To achieve this, I vary the type of interactions. In turn, I expect the students to actively participate.

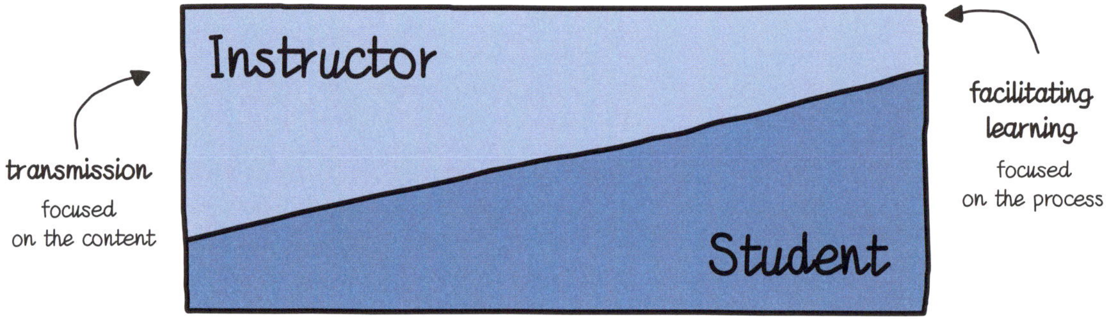

Use Students' Prior Knowledge and Skills...

Another important aspect when thinking about your teaching approach is your relationship to knowledge, and, in particular, how you intend to take into account the students' prior knowledge and skills. This relationship can be illustrated by the diagram above. The left-most position on the diagram shows a situation where the instructor believes that they master the content and that the students have basically no knowledge of the subject, or that the instructor does not wish to call upon the understanding they may have. In this situation, the instructor is the content expert.

At the other end of the diagram, the instructor believes that the students have a broad knowledge of the content and calls upon them during the course. The instructor in this case is a process expert, that is, they manage the questions and strategies to allow students to best express their knowledge and skills.

It is important to emphasize that this is a continuum, and even though individually we might favor a particular position, this position is dynamic; it will change during a course, as well as from one course to another.

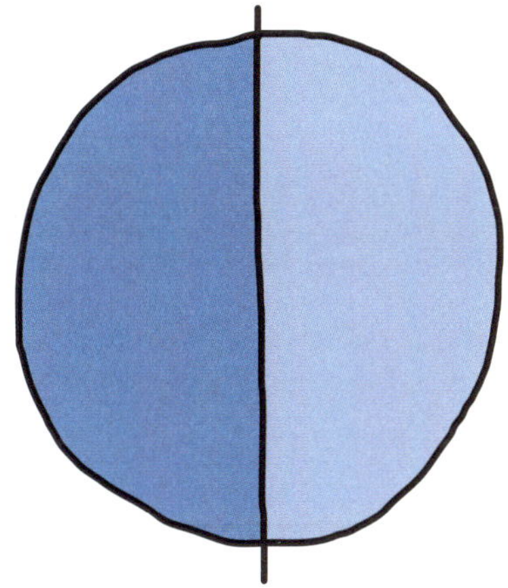

... and Clarify Roles by Means of a Teaching Contract

You can present your teaching philosophy for a given course using a teaching contract. One aspect of the contract allows you to clearly state how the class will be organized and how it will function. Another aspect establishes the roles and expectations of both the instructor and the students to ensure that the two parties work together towards the same objective: building knowledge. Concretely, it can take the form of a table. Don't forget to specify what is expected not just in terms of the work itself but also the students' attitudes.

More broadly, this table conveys the message that learning is a kind of co-construction: each participant must fulfill their obligations in order to achieve the learning outcomes.

14 17

Instructor	Student
Present the theoretical elements as a lecture while including concrete examples from daily life to illustrate the concept (class on Thursday afternoon).	Actively listen, take notes, ask questions when clarification is needed. Go over notes prior to each class. Write down questions to ask the instructor or other students to clarify understanding of certain concepts.
Prepare class exercises to further develop the concepts that have been presented. Reply to student questions during the exercise session. Provide group feedback at the end of the exercise.	Complete the exercises, ask questions when clarification is needed. Take group feedback into account and adjust work as necessary.
Provide a list of reference books and scientific articles for the students to further study the concepts presented in class, along with a lecture schedule for the semester. Set up a discussion forum relating to the resources and reply to any questions that are asked (connect to the forum on Wednesday morning). Take time at the start of each class to go over any issues that have come up on the discussion forum.	Read items on the resource list in time according to the lecture schedule. Ensure that notes taken in class include the key elements. Ask questions on the discussion forum (up until Tuesday evening each week). Interact with other students and/or answer questions asked on the forum.
Include a 10-minute break between two hours of class time.	Stick to the allotted break time.

The work you have completed in this section will help you clarify your teaching vision and, along with the work in the "Develop" section of the book, prepare your teaching portfolio.

Design

The design section is intended to guide you through the various phases of course development. We have suggested a progressive approach that goes from the concept map to the final scenario and that respects constructive alignment.

At the Heart of the Book Lies the Principle of Constructive Alignment...

According to the principle of constructive alignment described in the literature, you should envisage the teaching process as a coherent whole that includes three key elements: the intended learning outcomes, the teaching and learning strategy, and the assessment strategy.

In this book, we also emphasize two other elements, which, although mentioned in the literature, have not been sufficiently expanded on—content and context. In our experience providing teaching support to instructors, we have often discussed the issue of content: How do I best transmit content to my students? How do I select the content so that it is at the correct level for my students? Given that the aim of this book is to help guide you toward a student-centered approach without sidelining content, the very foundation of teaching, including it was an obvious step. The point is, after all, to think about ways of helping students take ownership of the course content!

Constructive alignment enables us to clearly establish what learning experience we want to offer our students. It also allows us to make our teaching choices explicit, which can be useful for sharing them with colleagues who may or may not be directly involved in teaching, or for giving students a key to understanding the reasons behind the learning activities.

Designing a course in line with the principles of constructive alignment therefore involves clearly expressing your teaching intentions instead of leaving them in the form of an intuition. The idea is to shift from intuition to intention!

For example, if your aim is to improve students' skill at presenting oral arguments [ILO], alignment means that your learning activities must enable them to develop this skill during the course (through peer discussions, debates, class presentations, etc.) and your assessment strategy must involve some form of oral exam. This may seem obvious, but there are often discrepancies between the intended outcome and the activities proposed or the assessment method.

4 5 8 9

... and the Canvas

To put into effect the principle of constructive alignment, we have developed a canvas that comprises five building blocks. These should be considered as one coherent whole.

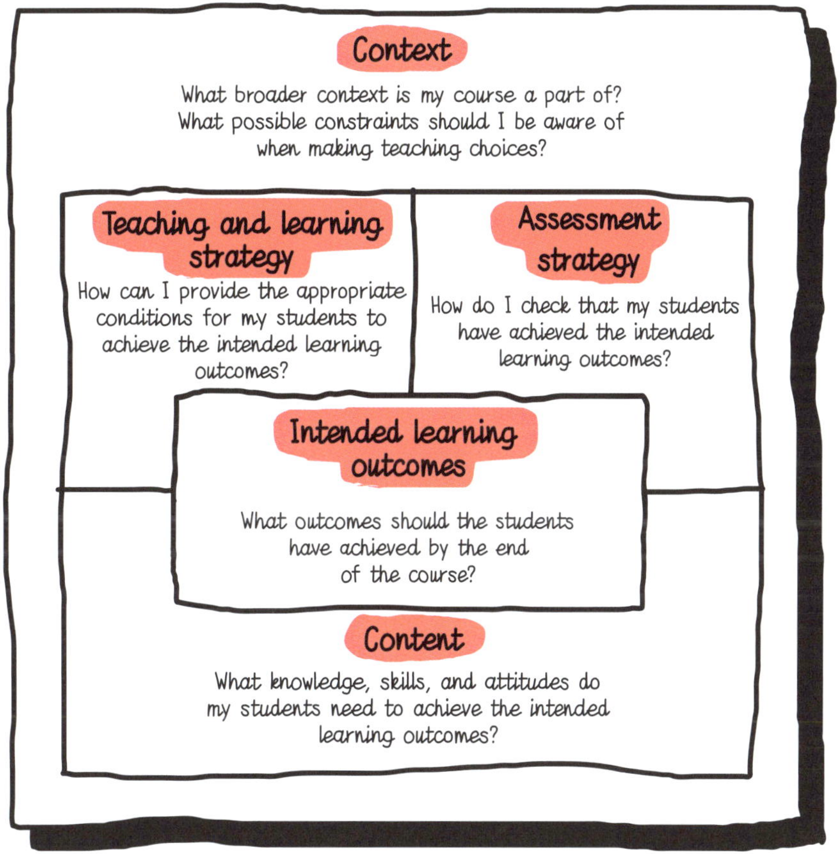

A Systemic Approach

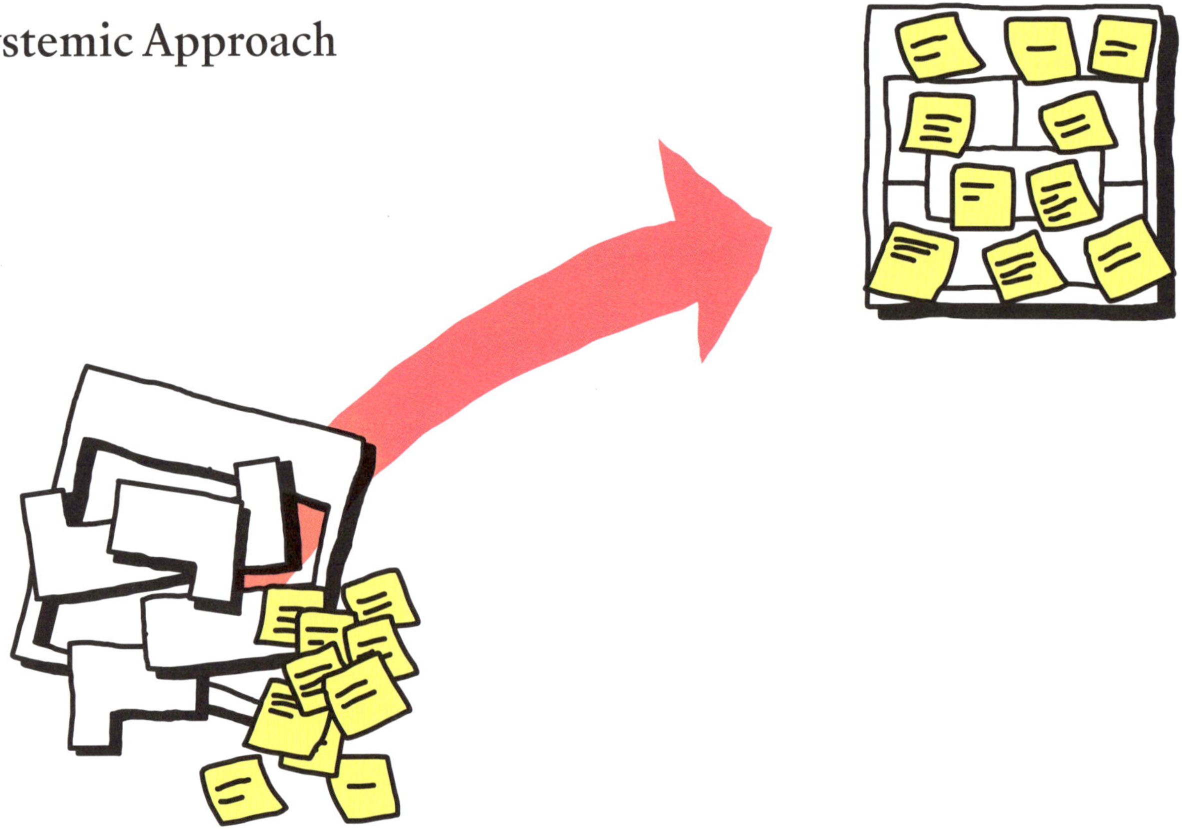

You must test the coherence between each building block to check that the course you are designing corresponds with the learning experience you wish to provide to students. The arrows illustrate the systemic aspect of this thought process, namely that each component influences the other.

In the following pages we have put forward a series of activities that will allow you to fill out the canvas and test the alignment of the course you are developing. The canvas is the book's main tool, and it gives structure to your thinking around teaching. It is based on the principles of constructive alignment, that is, the need to ensure consistency between the four cornerstones of any course: intended learning outcomes (ILOs), content, teaching and learning strategy, and assessment strategy, which are all influenced by a given context (the fifth cornerstone). The canvas helps structure the process of creating or redesigning a course. It allows you to think about the choices relating to each of the four building blocks, as well as to the overall alignment of the course, which is the ultimate goal.

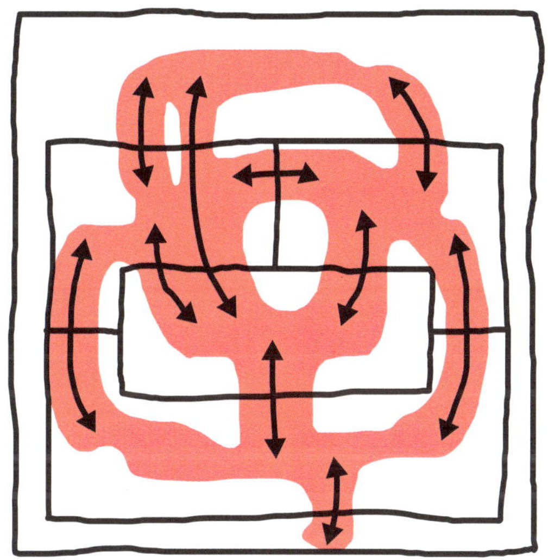

The Five Building Blocks of the Canvas in Detail

Context

Every course is always part of a specific context, which includes factors relating to the students (number, diversity, etc.), the wider curriculum (year of study, number of credits assigned to the course, etc.), and resources available to the instructor (classroom size, material, available funding, etc.), as well as factors relating to the instructor (familiarity with certain teaching methods, available teaching time, etc.). The context can have a positive or negative effect on the teaching choices that the instructor will make.

Intended learning outcomes

In the center of the canvas we have the learning outcomes. Here you must define the outcomes you wish the students to achieve by the end of the course. These learning outcomes are useful for the instructor because they help build the course, communicate expectations to the students, and assess whether the students have successfully integrated the knowledge, skills, and attitudes the course was designed to convey. The learning outcomes will also be useful for students because they clearly outline the targets to be achieved and what is expected in terms of learning.

Content

The content is the foundation upon which the course is built, and the instructor is an expert in the content. As an instructor, your work involves choosing and structuring the content that you believe is relevant for students, depending on the learning context (e.g., available teaching time, student level, etc.) and the ILOs.

Teaching and learning strategy

The teaching and learning strategy includes all the learning activities presented to the students to allow them to achieve the learning outcomes. It is not a question here of the teaching formats (e.g., lectures, tutorials, etc.) but of the actual activities (e.g., case studies, peer discussions, class presentations, etc.) proposed as part of these formats.

Assessment strategy

The assessment strategy involves activities to be carried out by students so they can receive feedback on their learning and check whether they have achieved the ILOs. It may include marked or unmarked exercises, exams, reports to be handed in, oral presentations, etc. It may comprise formative assessments (giving feedback on student work) or summative assessments (giving a grade for student work).

Seven Steps to Complete your Canvas

Whether you're starting from scratch or wanting to check your course alignment, we suggest you follow these seven steps.

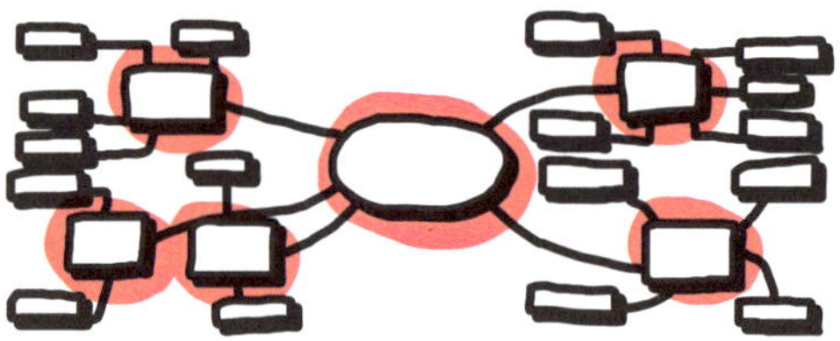

1. Identify the key concepts in your course

2. Identify the contextual aspects that influence your course

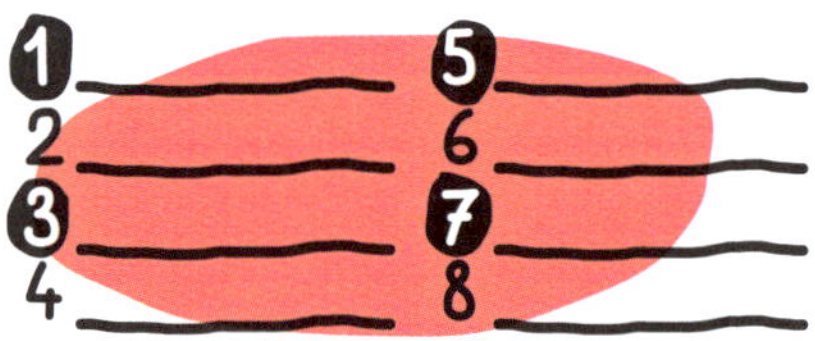

3. Write down the intended learning outcomes for your course

4. Clarify and select the content for your course

5. **Formulate your teaching and learning strategy**

6. **Formulate your assessment strategy**

7. **Create a scenario for how your course will unfold**

I. Identifying the Key Concepts in Your Course

What are the key concepts that must be covered?

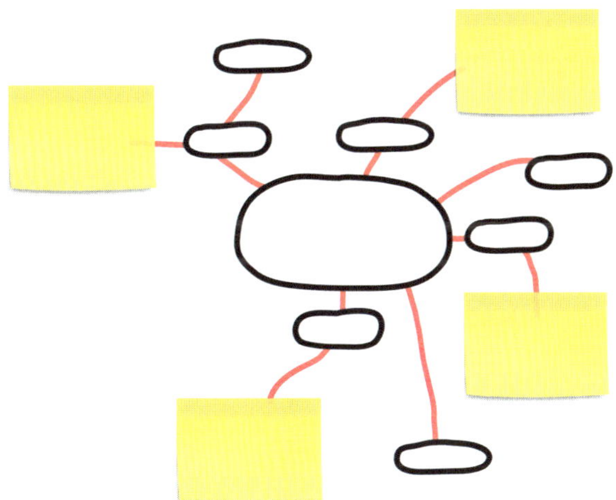

Identify the Key Concepts by Drawing Up a Concept Map

The first step involves identifying the key concepts you want to convey. You can also choose to begin with the ILOs, however, study of actual practice shows that in most cases, instructors start this thought process with the content.

During this first step, we suggest drawing a concept map to highlight the key concepts in your course.

Example of a concept map:

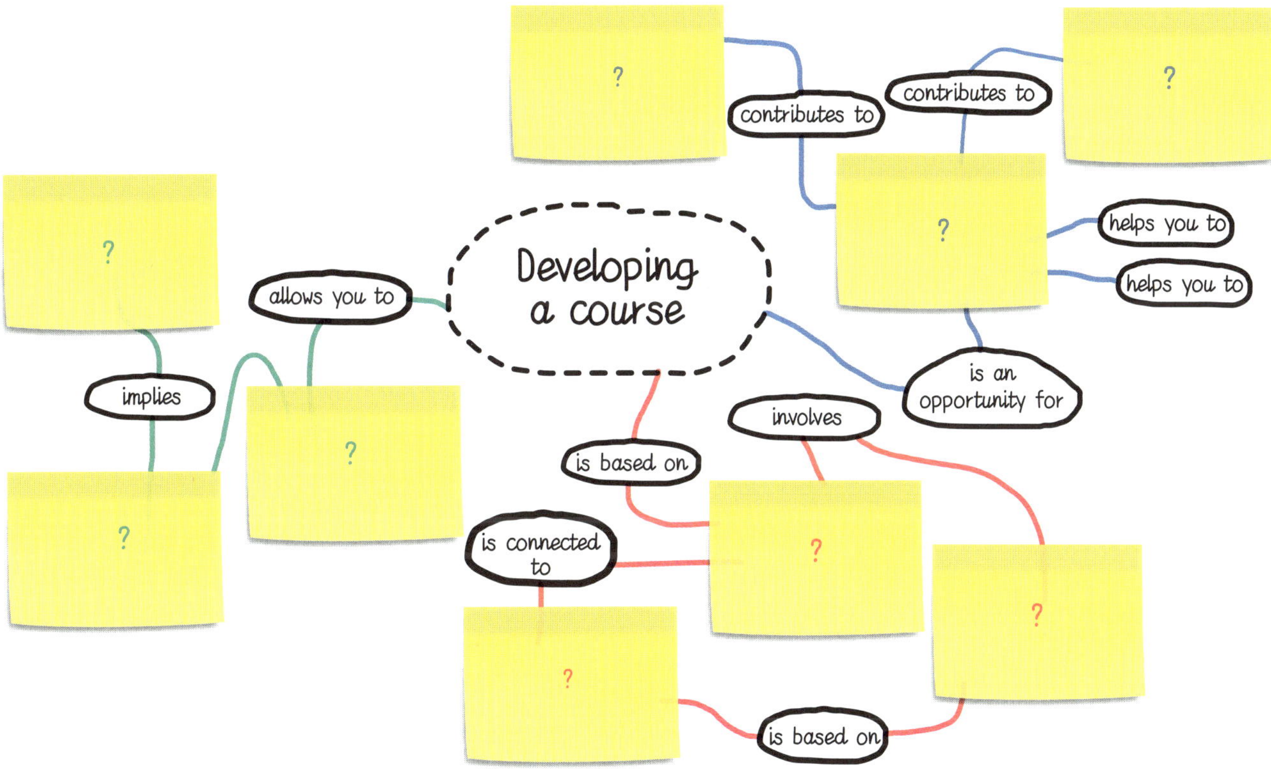

What are the key concepts you want to convey?

Why Create a Concept Map?

A concept map, sometimes called a "mind map," is a structured visual representation that provides an overview of the conceptual network of a specific topic. It enables a concept to be positioned within a relational network connecting it to other concepts and knowledge.

A concept map allows you to relate the various elements of a course to each other, one by one. It can help you identify the most important concepts, clarify the relationships between them, and focus on the key elements of the content.

A concept map can also be used to present the course structure to students, help them develop their understanding around a concept, or visualize the relationships between various elements covered in the course. You could also ask students to produce a concept map at the beginning or end of a course to get an idea of how they see the topic.

Concept Map for the Book

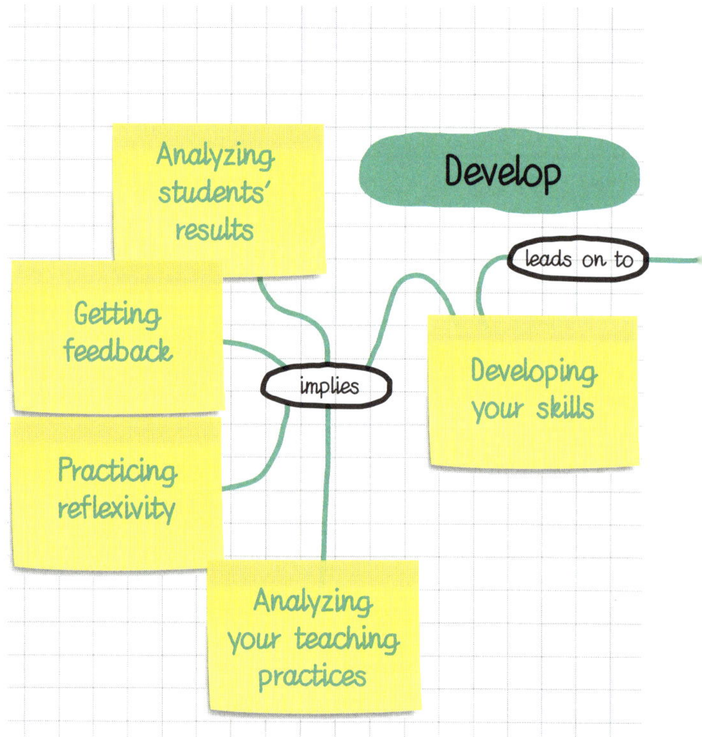

10 11

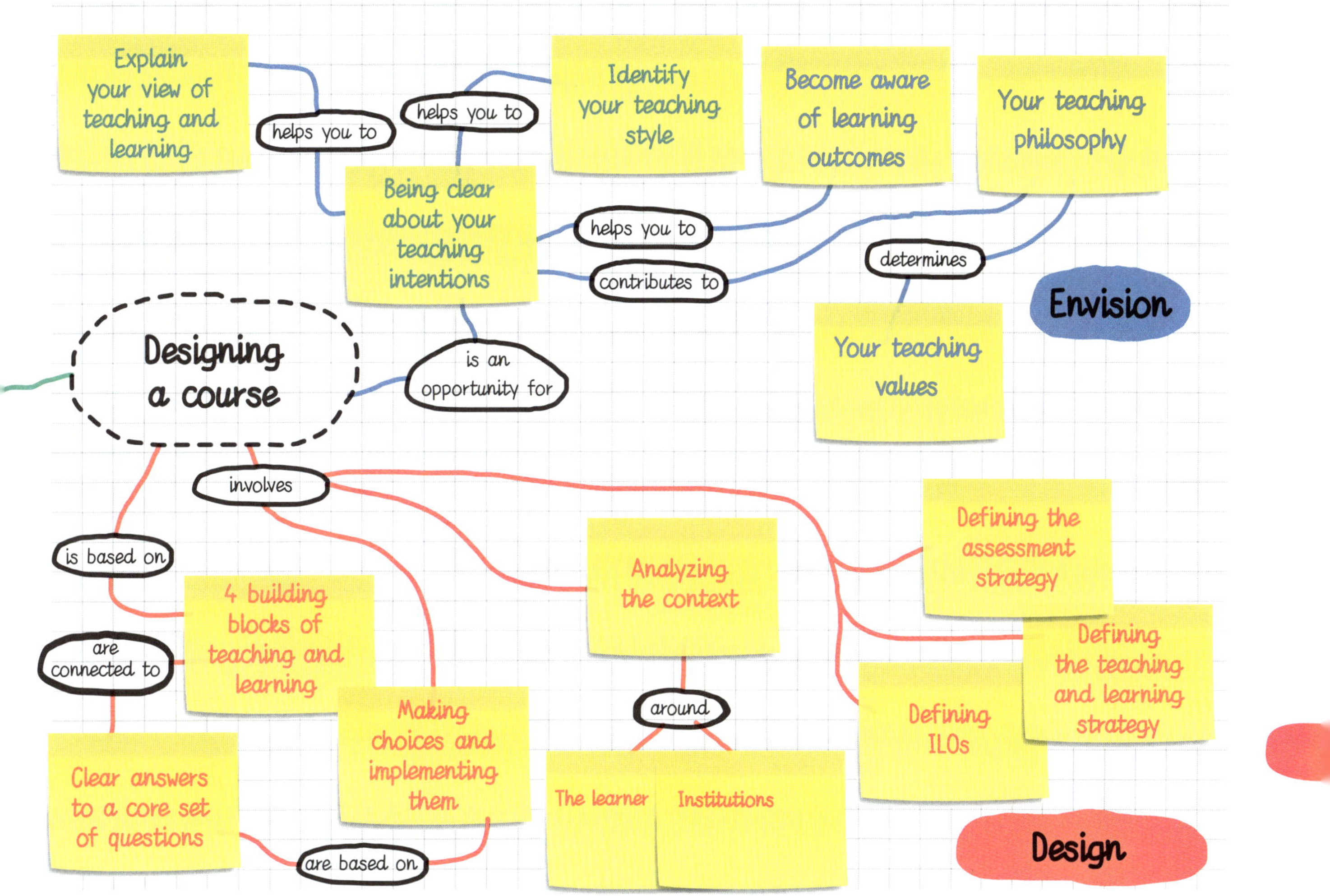
Explain your view of teaching and learning
helps you to
helps you to
Identify your teaching style
Become aware of learning outcomes
Your teaching philosophy
Being clear about your teaching intentions
helps you to
contributes to
determines
Envision
Designing a course
is an opportunity for
Your teaching values
involves
is based on
4 building blocks of teaching and learning
are connected to
Clear answers to a core set of questions
Making choices and implementing them
are based on
Analyzing the context
around
The learner
Institutions
Defining the assessment strategy
Defining the teaching and learning strategy
Defining ILOs
Design

Preparing the First Draft of Your Concept Map

Using the steps below, now try your own concept map.

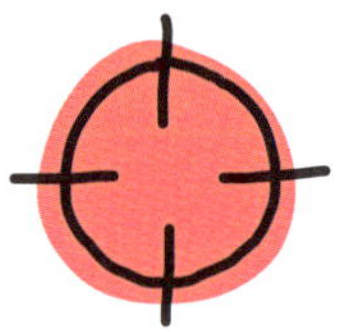

1 Identify the topic or main concept for the map.

2 Draw up a list of 20 to 30 concepts that must be covered in the course you are designing.

3 From this list, identify the 10 or 15 most important concepts.

4 Write each concept on a sticky note.

5 Place the concepts on a blank sheet of paper and position them in relation to one another.

6 Establish the relationships between the concepts and name them.

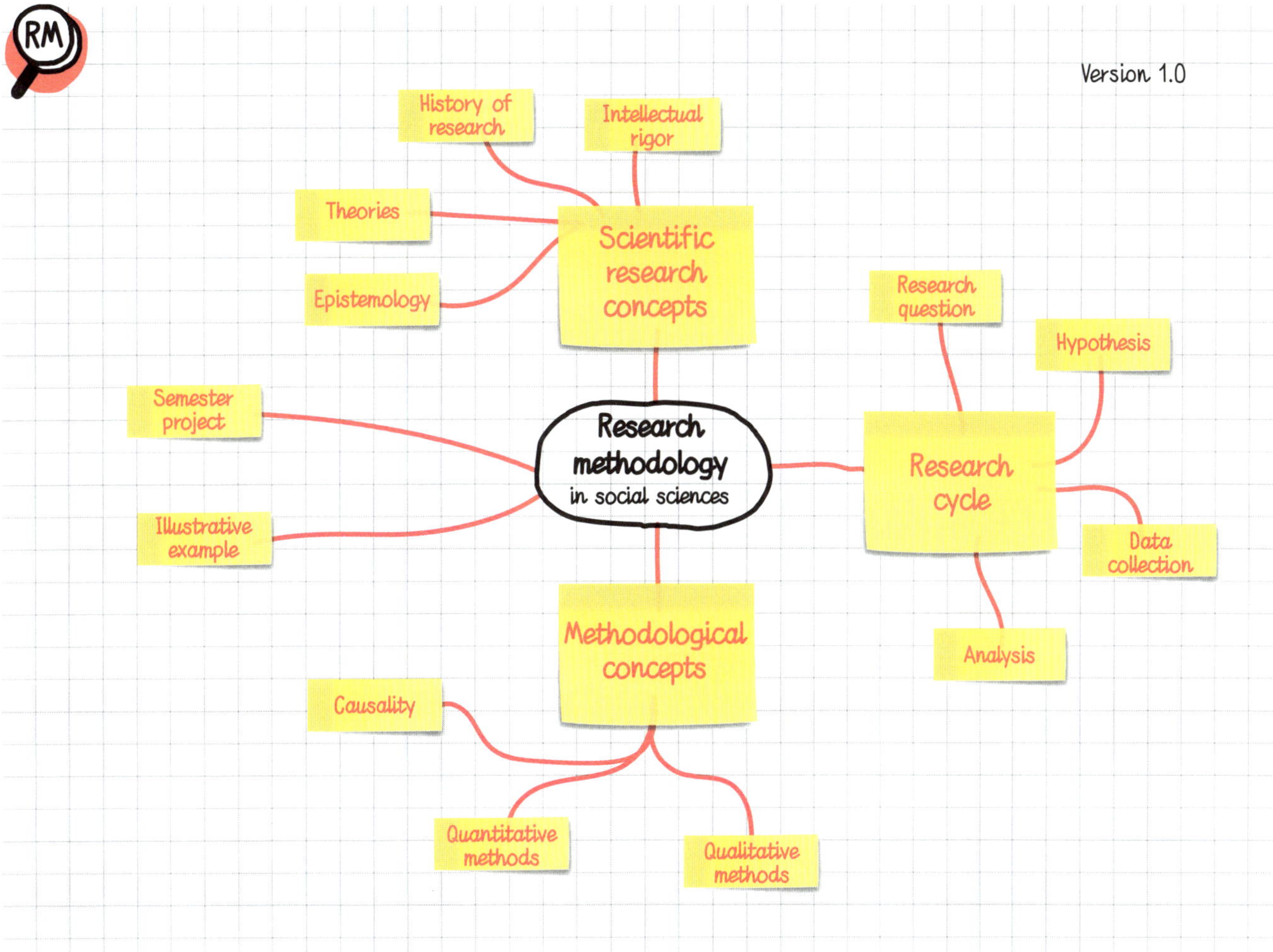
RM
Version 1.0
History of research
Intellectual rigor
Theories
Epistemology
Scientific research concepts
Research question
Hypothesis
Semester project
Research methodology in social sciences
Research cycle
Illustrative example
Data collection
Methodological concepts
Analysis
Causality
Quantitative methods
Qualitative methods

Expanding on Your First Draft

Using your first draft as a basis, develop and expand on your map with these three actions:

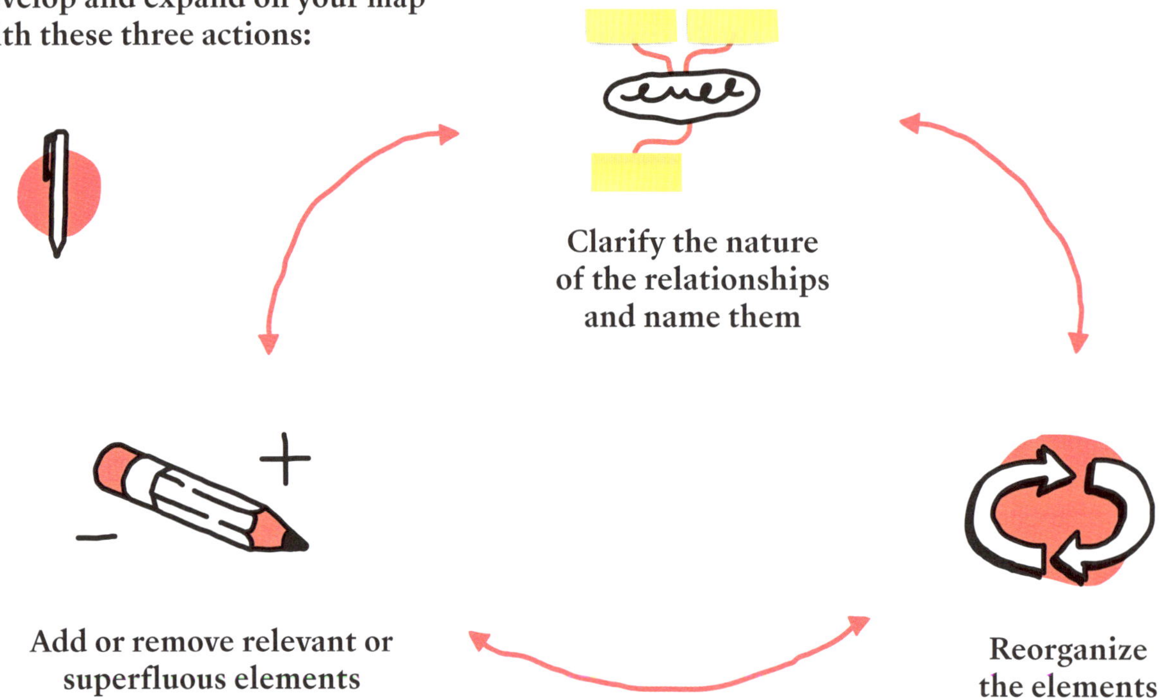

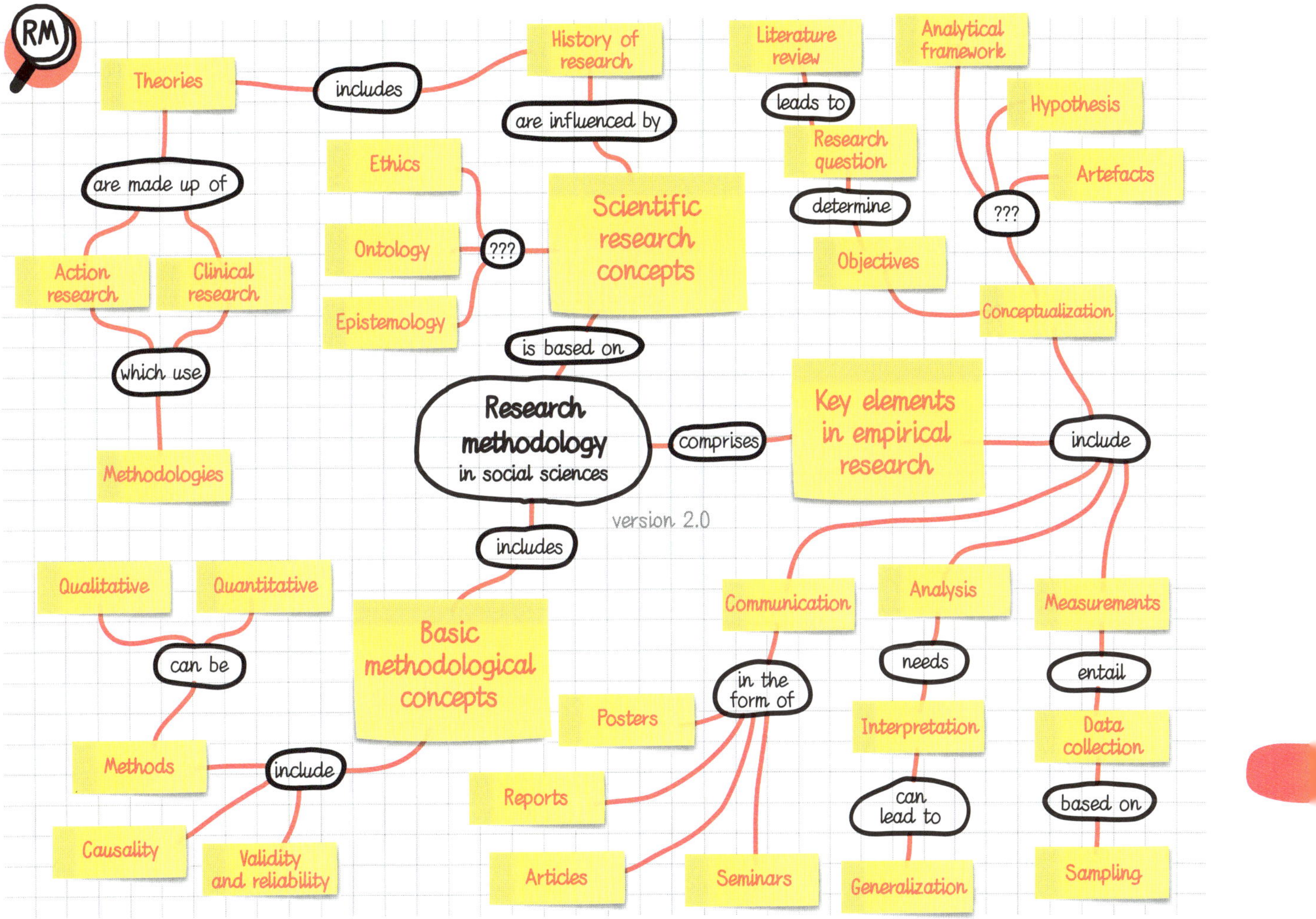
RM
Research methodology in social sciences
version 2.0
is based on
Scientific research concepts
are influenced by
History of research
includes
Theories
are made up of
Action research
Clinical research
which use
Methodologies
Ethics
Ontology
Epistemology
???
Literature review
leads to
Research question
determine
Objectives
Analytical framework
Hypothesis
Artefacts
???
Conceptualization
comprises
Key elements in empirical research
include
Communication
in the form of
Posters
Reports
Articles
Seminars
Analysis
needs
Interpretation
can lead to
Generalization
Measurements
entail
Data collection
based on
Sampling
includes
Basic methodological concepts
include
Methods
can be
Qualitative
Quantitative
Causality
Validity and reliability

Checking Over Your Concept Map

Refer to the questions below to analyze your map and make sure it clearly reflects the most important concepts and the connections between them. The map should be self-explanatory.

- ☐ Can the main concept be identified easily?
- ☐ Is the map easily understandable as a whole?
- ☐ Do the concepts illustrated on the map provide an overview of the topic in question?
- ☐ Are the most important concepts clearly visible?
- ☐ Are the most important concepts connected to the main topic in a clear manner?
- ☐ Are the connections between the concepts understandable?
- ☐ Does the content you have selected enable you to plan out your intended course?
- ☐ Can the map be handed out to students to give them an overview of the content that will be covered in the course?

Now that you have checked over your concept map, you will be better able to translate the key concepts into ILOs and content.

But before that, you must define the contextual elements in which the course takes place.

II. Identifying the Key Contextual Elements That Influence the Course

What broader context is my course a part of?
What possible constraints should I be aware of when making teaching and learning choices?

The Context Affects Teaching Choices

A course always takes place within a specific context, and so different contextual elements can potentially add constraints when designing your course.

These may be material or immaterial. How many students will there be? Can the tables in the classroom be moved? At what moment in the day or week will the course take place? What are the institutional rules and practices regarding teaching? Will I have to teach some or all of the course via distance learning?

The context can have a varying degree of influence on the intended learning outcomes, content, teaching and learning strategy, and assessment strategy.

Furthermore, much of the context is out of the instructor's hands. This is therefore an opportunity to identify the contextual aspects that will influence your teaching choices, starting from these four categories.

Students

How many students are there?
How familiar are the students with the teaching approaches I intend to use?
What knowledge, skills, and attitudes do the students already have?
How diverse is my group of students?

Resources

What is the teaching space like (classroom furniture and size)?
What materials do I have available?
What teaching resources can I access for this course?
What financial resources are available?

Curriculum

What is the planned teaching format (lectures, practical work, seminars, etc.)?
How many credits are allocated to this course?
How does this course fit in with others in the curriculum?
What is the level of this course (Bachelor's, Master's, continuing education, etc.)?
Does this course have a limit to the number of students that can pass?
Are the ILOs already set?
What are the institutional rules and practices?
Is this a compulsory or optional course?

Instructors

Are other instructors or assistants involved in this course?
What feedback (from students, colleagues, exam results) is available about this course?
What level of responsibility do I have for this course?
How much time do I have available to develop this course?
How comfortable am I with the subject and/or with certain teaching approaches?
What are my specific intentions for this course?

Sample Analysis of Context

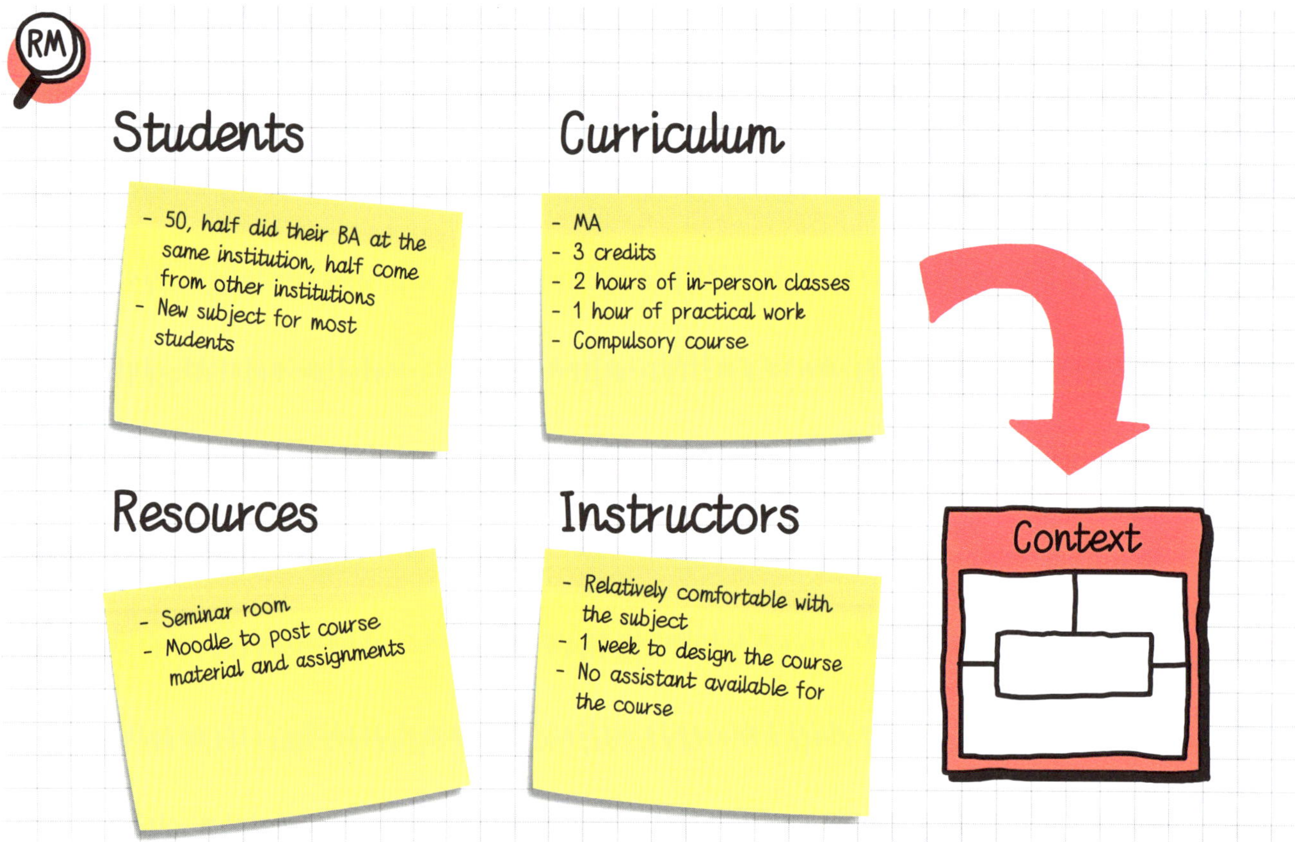

The instructor has identified all the contextual elements that might affect teaching choices. We can see that there is only one week available for course design, which will have an impact on how the instructor will structure the content, as well as to the activities they intend to deliver.

In this example, the instructor will have to think carefully about which elements of content to include. There will not be enough time to do a literature review to expand on or update the content, and the instructor will almost certainly be forced to reuse content that they are already comfortable with. It will also be difficult to create course handouts. However, it may be possible to ask the students to help create these handouts. For example, it would be entirely feasible to create a wiki on Moodle and every week designate a group of students to create this content together, under the supervision of the instructor.

In terms of the teaching and learning strategy, the instructor should also use activities that the students are already familiar with. The instructor will also have to consider the large class size and come up with activities that are easy to manage and for which feedback can be provided. Peer review could be employed here, whereby students are provided with a rubric for reviewing other students' tasks. This will give students some initial feedback that they can use to improve their work.

Aligning the Course with the Curriculum

Other courses that form part of the curriculum are a vital element of the context and must be taken into account as much as possible, bearing in mind that each course will have its own priorities.

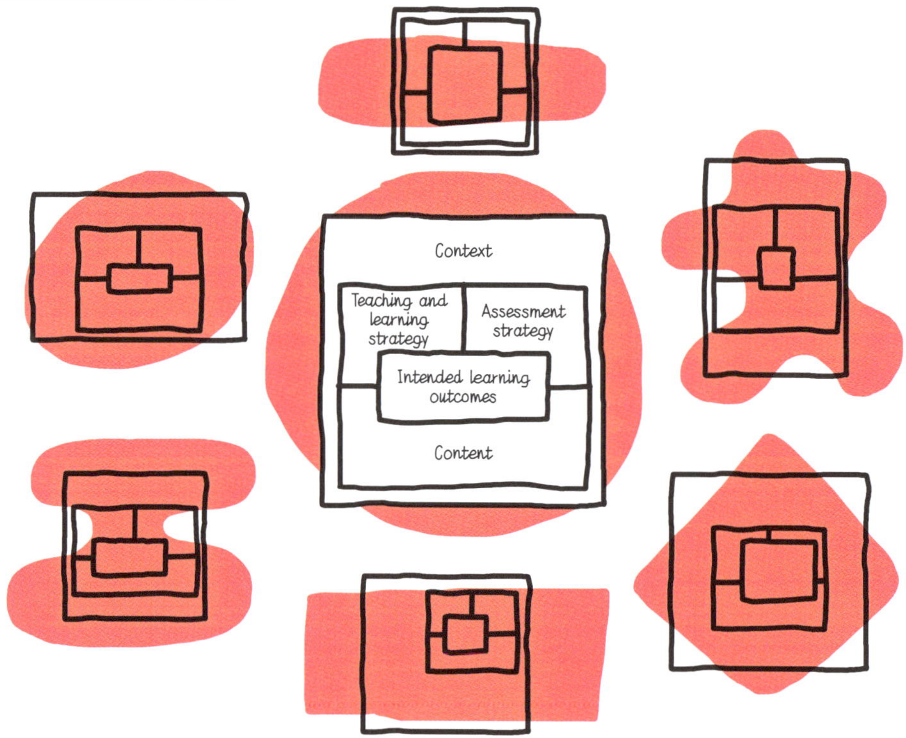

Clearly Defining the Context

Go back to your canvas and complete the “Context” box. We recommend writing down on sticky notes the elements that might affect your teaching approaches (1 sticky note per element).

Students

Curriculum

Resources

Instructors

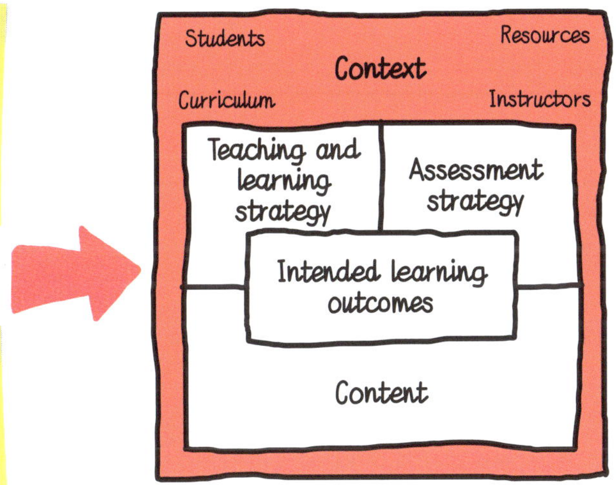

III. Formulating the Intended Learning Outcomes for Your Course

What ILOs should the students have achieved by the end of the course?

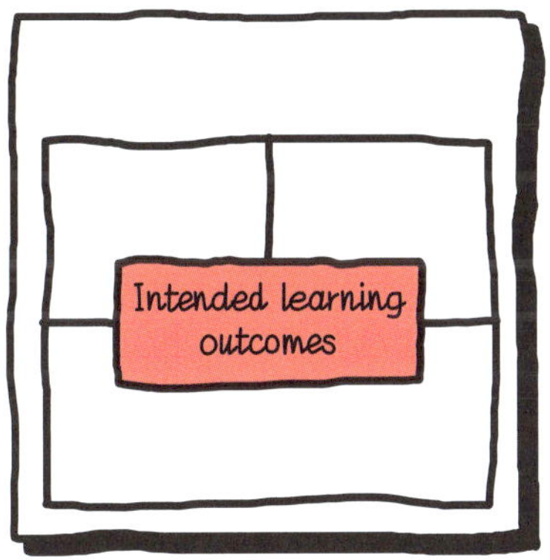

The Importance of Learning Outcomes

Clearly defining the ILOs will enable you to pinpoint the learning (knowledge, skills, and attitudes) that the students should have acquired by the end of the course.

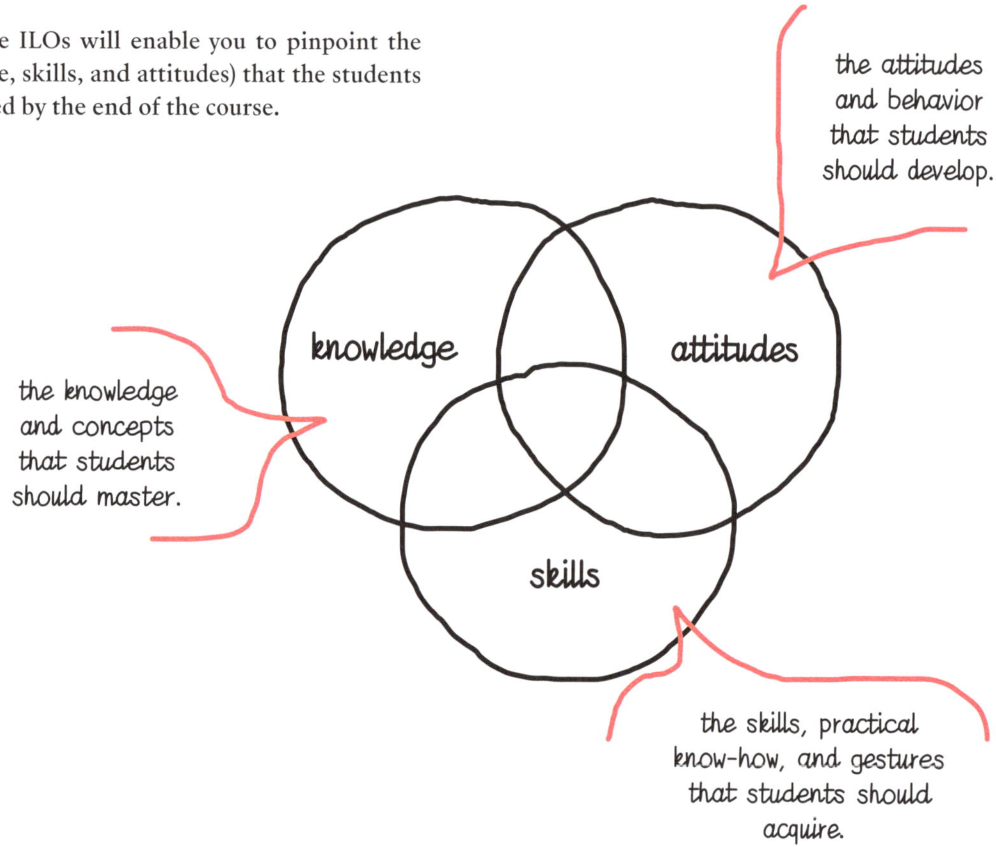

24 25

The ILOs will help you **construct** your course. They are at the center of the constructive alignment canvas because they serve as the basis for your choice of teaching and learning activities.

These learning outcomes are also used to **communicate** to students what you want them to learn. This allows them to be clear about what is expected of them and then do the necessary work.

Finally, the ILOs allow you to clarify what aspects you need to **assess.** By establishing clear goals for what you expect students to have integrated by the end of the course, it becomes easier to identify the best methods for assessment and what the assessment will focus on.

The ILOs also allow you to determine the level of mastery you expect the students to have attained by the end of the course, which could range from simple memorization of concepts (surface learning) to the integration of concepts into the student's understanding (deep learning). Deep learning means that the students will retain knowledge on a more permanent basis and will be able to apply it in various situations, while surface learning means that the student can access knowledge relating to very specific situations and on a more temporary basis.

Deep learning requires more time, so you should make sure that the time you allocate for each ILO is appropriate for the number of course credits.

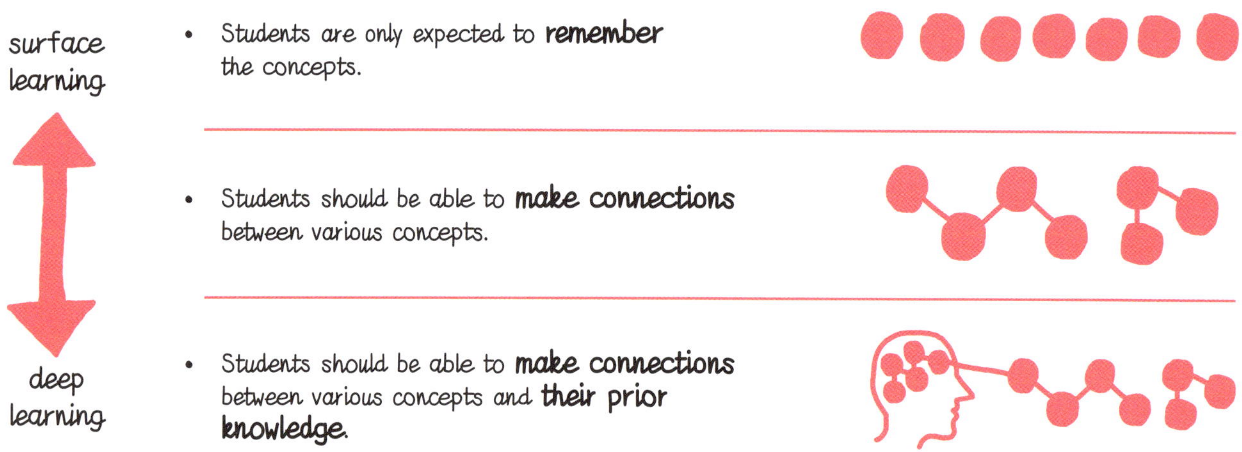

Establishing and Formulating Intended Learning Outcomes

ILOs should always include:

- An action verb that defines the level and type of intended learning;
- The learning content; and
- Any additional information that describes the situation within which the student must complete the task.

apply ethical standards to one's work

Make sure you don't confuse "learning outcomes" with "learning objectives," which relate to the instructor's objectives.

Teaching objectives or intentions	What the instructor envisages for content and course delivery, what they intend to do during the course.	Introduce students to ethical thinking on research
Learning outcomes	What the students should be able to do with the content, once the learning experience is completed (course, semester, year, etc.).	Apply ethical standards to one's work

Establishing the Type and Level of ILOs

Using an action verb will allow you to write ILOs that relate directly to student behavior (which will in turn help students achieve them) rather than to your teaching objective. Afterwards, it will also be easier to define your expectations around assessment of the ILOs. The students will better understand what is required to demonstrate achievement of the outcome.

The diagram on the following page presents a series of action verbs that can be used depending on the types of learning (knowledge, skills, attitudes) and the desired level of understanding (surface learning – deep learning).

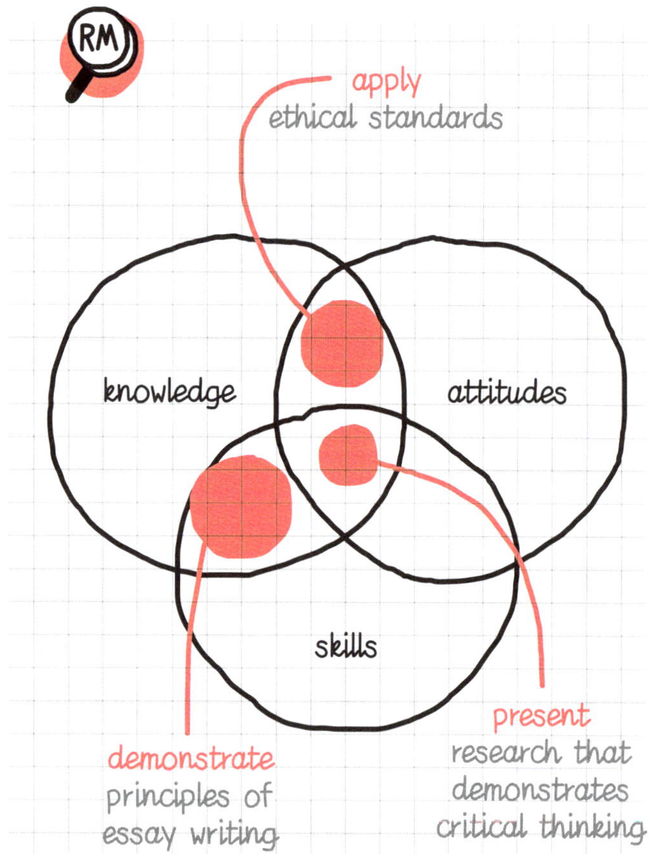

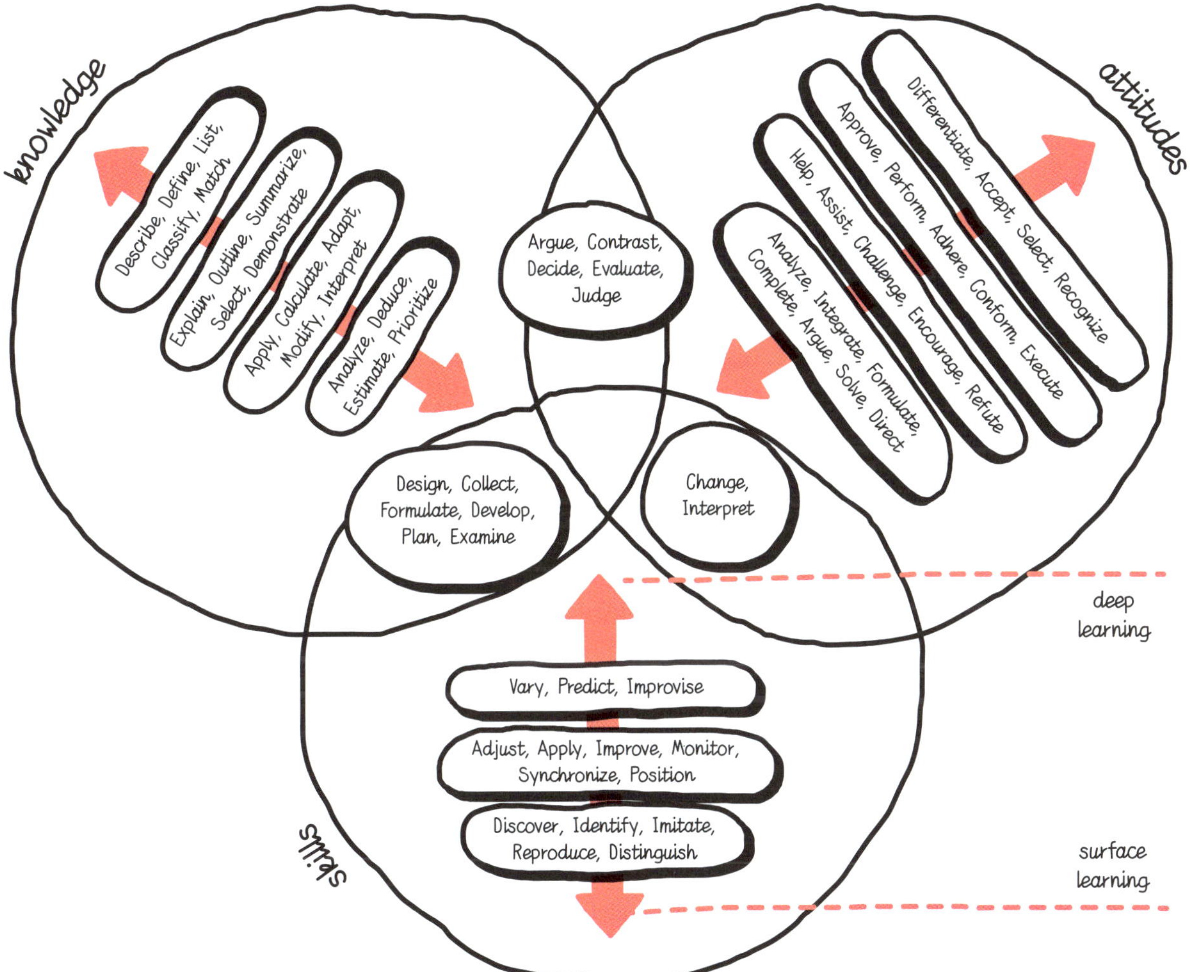
knowledge
Describe, Define, List, Classify, Match
Explain, Outline, Summarize, Select, Demonstrate
Apply, Calculate, Adapt, Modify, Interpret
Analyze, Deduce, Estimate, Prioritize
attitudes
Differentiate, Accept, Select, Recognize
Approve, Perform, Adhere, Conform, Execute
Help, Assist, Challenge, Encourage, Refute
Analyze, Integrate, Formulate, Complete, Argue, Solve, Direct
Argue, Contrast, Decide, Evaluate, Judge
Design, Collect, Formulate, Develop, Plan, Examine
Change, Interpret
Vary, Predict, Improvise
Adjust, Apply, Improve, Monitor, Synchronize, Position
Discover, Identify, Imitate, Reproduce, Distinguish
skills
deep learning
surface learning

Identifying the ILOs That Students Should Achieve

Think carefully about the concepts you want the students to be able to employ at the end of the course. Which ones do you want to assess? Why?

This may relate to knowledge, skills, or attitudes and must align with the teaching and learning content.

In the university context, there is a tendency to focus on "knowledge" outcomes, but it may be more appropriate to incorporate other learning content into your course, for example, to encourage students to adopt an ethical stance, work together as a team, debate a point, etc.

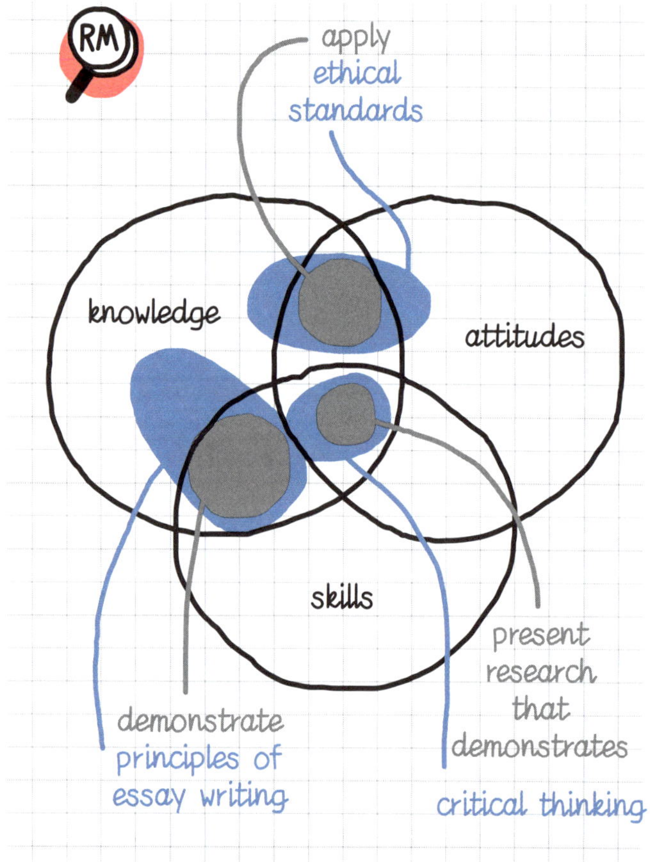

Specifying the Situation in Which Students Demonstrate Their Learning

Lastly, proof that the learning outcome has been achieved must be observable in a specific situation. This requires you to clearly define the context within which the knowledge, skills, or attitudes will be used.

Introducing additional information will allow you to specify the conditions within which students will perform the task. This will also make it easier to control how the learning outcome is achieved.

RM

apply ethical standards to one's work

The situation in which students perform the task will affect the ILOs, as in the below examples. Similar elements of content can be observed in various situations and can be employed to achieve different levels of understanding. This will allow you, for example, to distinguish between topics that are similar but are aimed at different levels of study.

RM

2nd year Bachelor's	1st year Master's
• Recognize ethical standards in scientific research	• Apply ethical standards to one's work
• Describe the principles of essay writing in a scientific article	• Demonstrate the principles of essay writing in a research report
• Recognize the ethical implications in research involving living beings	• Critically assess the ethical implications of a research project

Making Sure the ILOs Are Clearly Expressed

The three previous steps will allow you to establish the main elements of your learning outcomes. In order to verify the quality of these outcomes and their ability to construct, communicate, and assess, you must make sure the following criteria have been fulfilled:

- **Student-Centered**
  Make sure the outcomes are focused on student learning. When writing the outcomes, keep this prompt in mind: "At the end of my course, the students will be able to..."
- **Clear**
  One idea per learning outcome
- **Aligned with content**
  Obvious connection with course content
- **Observable**
  The students must be able to prove they have achieved the outcome
- **Situation-based**
  The situation is clearly specified

RM

- Demonstrate the principles of essay writing and familiarity with bibliographic standards.

How do you assess "familiarity with bibliographic standards"? You will have to reformulate this outcome to clarify exactly what you expect the student to accomplish:

- Demonstrate the principles of essay writing in a research report and respect bibliographic standards when writing a research report. 1/2

However, this outcome now includes two distinct learning outcomes. Instead write two separate outcomes as follows:

- Demonstrate the principles of essay writing in a research report.
- Respect bibliographic standards in a research report.

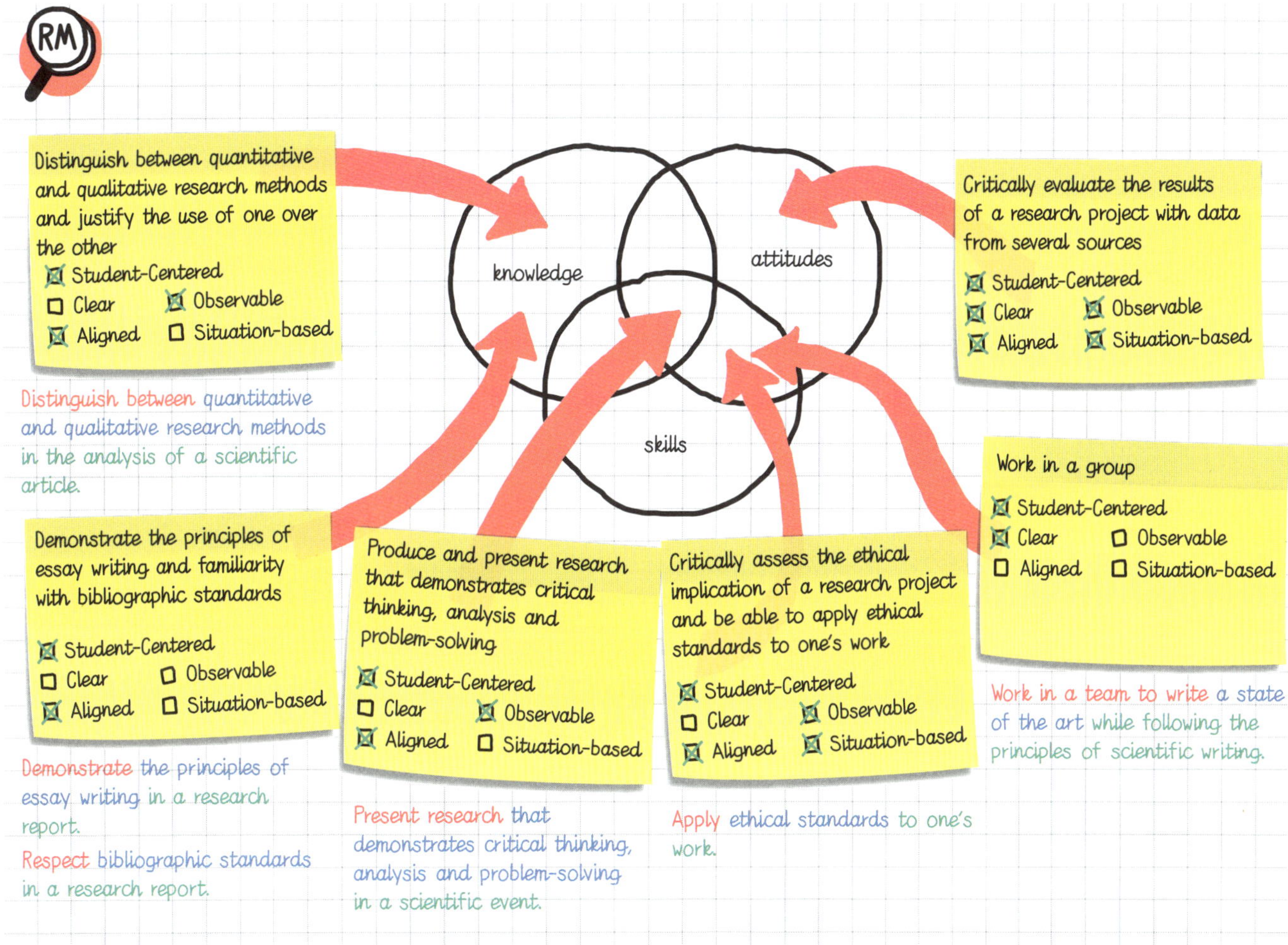
RM
knowledge
attitudes
skills
Distinguish between quantitative and qualitative research methods and justify the use of one over the other
☒ Student-Centered
☐ Clear ☒ Observable
☒ Aligned ☐ Situation-based
Distinguish between quantitative and qualitative research methods in the analysis of a scientific article.
Critically evaluate the results of a research project with data from several sources
☒ Student-Centered
☒ Clear ☒ Observable
☒ Aligned ☒ Situation-based
Work in a group
☒ Student-Centered
☒ Clear ☐ Observable
☐ Aligned ☐ Situation-based
Work in a team to write a state of the art while following the principles of scientific writing.
Demonstrate the principles of essay writing and familiarity with bibliographic standards
☒ Student-Centered
☐ Clear ☐ Observable
☒ Aligned ☐ Situation-based
Demonstrate the principles of essay writing in a research report.
Respect bibliographic standards in a research report.
Produce and present research that demonstrates critical thinking, analysis and problem-solving
☒ Student-Centered
☐ Clear ☒ Observable
☒ Aligned ☐ Situation-based
Present research that demonstrates critical thinking, analysis and problem-solving in a scientific event.
Critically assess the ethical implication of a research project and be able to apply ethical standards to one's work
☒ Student-Centered
☐ Clear ☒ Observable
☒ Aligned ☒ Situation-based
Apply ethical standards to one's work.

We suggest you use the following table to draft your learning outcomes.

	1. Define the type and level of understanding	2. Identify the learning outcome that must be achieved by the students	3. Clearly define the situation within which students will achieve the outcome
At the end of my course, the students will be able to:			

4. Make sure that each ILO is clearly expressed:

- ☐ Student-Centered
- ☐ Clear
- ☐ Aligned with content
- ☐ Observable
- ☐ Situation-based

Here are some contextual elements you should take into account when developing your learning outcomes:

- Are there any ILOs that have already been set?
- How many credits are available?
- Are there any institutional prerequisites?
- What prior knowledge do the students have?
- Is the course more theory-oriented or practical?

After you have drafted your learning outcomes and checked their quality, write them on some sticky notes and place them on your canvas.

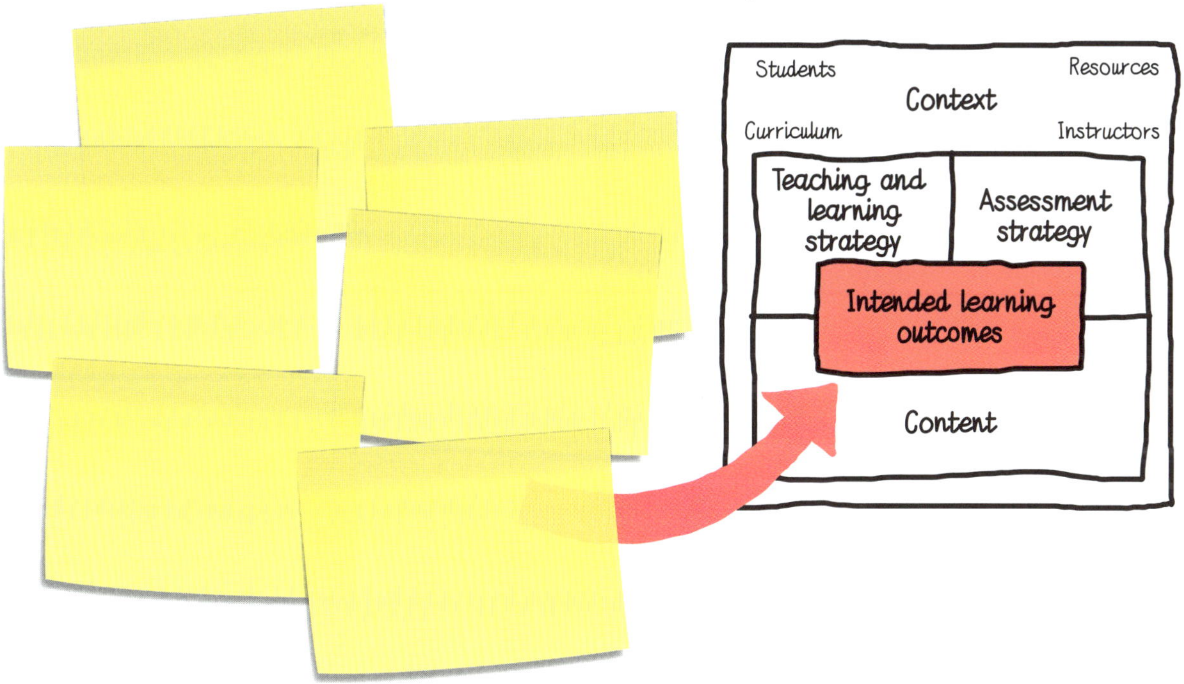

IV. Clarifying and Selecting Course Content

What knowledge, skills, and attitudes do my students need to achieve the ILOs?

Clarifying the Content

The notion of content encompasses many different aspects such as knowledge, know-how, or values—everything that is learned. In higher education, of course, there is often an emphasis on knowledge and understanding, usually related to the specific academic discipline. However, content can also include skills that may be more practical (e.g., laboratory procedures) or cognitive (e.g., problem-solving). The development of values and attitudes (e.g., intellectual rigor or scientific integrity) also forms part of content. In short, different types of content learned can be embedded and used in real-life situations. For example, students working on a team project need to be able to understand the methodology used in project management, use the relevant software, know how to communicate, and know how to manage conflict, among other things.

A Matrix to Visualize the Links between Content and ILOs

Given that ILOs are the cornerstone of teaching, it is important to ensure that the content is not chosen for its own sake but is clearly connected to them. A matrix can help you check this.

This table comprises ILOs (rows) and content (columns). Each cell allows you to identify the intersections and how well the content is spread across the ILOs; several different elements of content may relate to the same outcome or one element of content may relate to several outcomes.

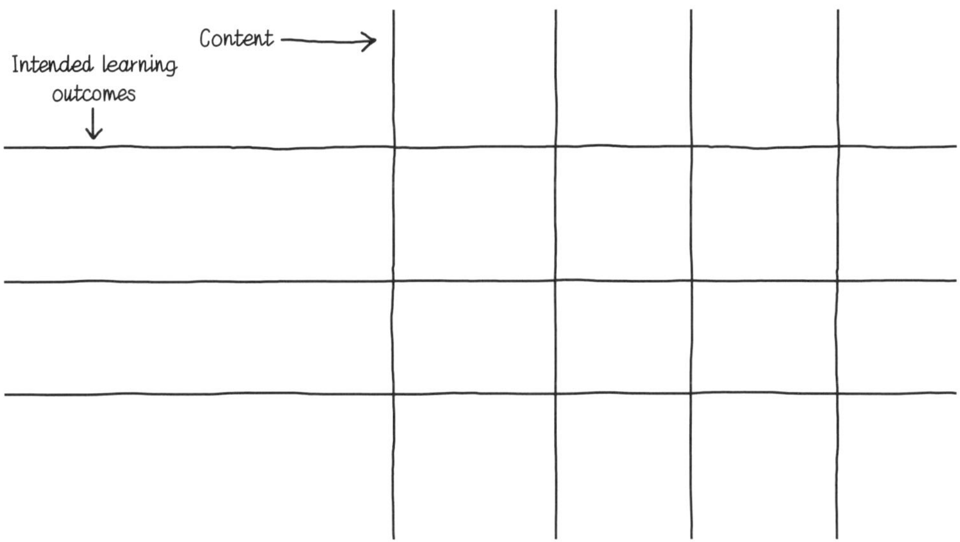

Identifying the Elements of Content from Your Concept Map

Although we sometimes feel a need to try and teach everything, it is important to establish priorities and make choices. The type and quantity of content that we transmit depends on several factors including available time, the level of the students, etc.

Intended learning outcomes ↓ / Content →	Research cycle and plan	Research ethics	Quantitative, qualitative, and mixed methods	Scientific writing

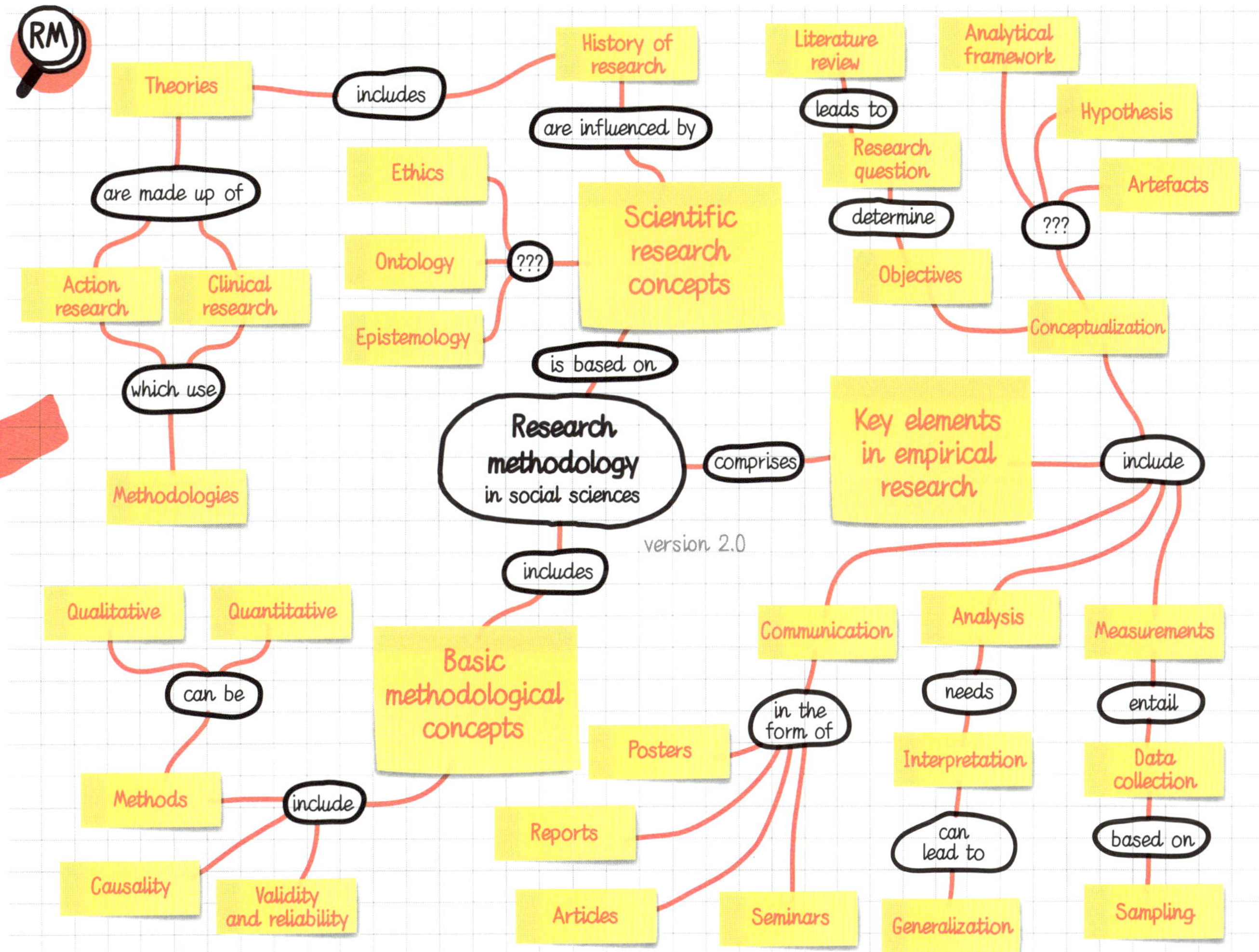
RM
Research methodology in social sciences
version 2.0
is based on
Scientific research concepts
are influenced by
History of research
includes
Theories
are made up of
Action research
Clinical research
which use
Methodologies
Ethics
Ontology
Epistemology
???
comprises
Key elements in empirical research
include
Literature review
leads to
Research question
determine
Objectives
Analytical framework
Hypothesis
Artefacts
???
Conceptualization
Communication
in the form of
Posters
Reports
Articles
Seminars
Analysis
needs
Interpretation
can lead to
Generalization
Measurements
entail
Data collection
based on
Sampling
includes
Basic methodological concepts
include
Methods
Causality
Validity and reliability
can be
Qualitative
Quantitative

Identifying the Connections between Elements of Content and the ILOs

To help you gain a comprehensive overview of your teaching content and its relationship to various ILOs, we suggest you make your own matrix.

Simply draw up a table like the one below. List the ILOs you have established in the rows and the main elements of content you have identified through your concept map (or any other form of analysis) in the columns.

Once you have built your matrix, identify the cells where there is an outcome/content intersection. This simply means going down each column and putting a cross in the rows where the ILO relates to that content.

version 1.0

Learning outcomes ↓ / Content →	Research cycle and plan	Research ethics	Quantitative, qualitative, and mixed methods	Scientific writing
Apply ethical standards to one's work		X		
Demonstrate the principles of essay writing in a research report				X
Critically evaluate the results of a research project and data from several sources				
Distinguish between quantitative and qualitative research methods in the analysis of a scientific article			X	
Present research that demonstrates critical thinking, analysis and problem-solving in a scientific event				X
Work in a team to write a state of the art while following the principles of scientific writing				X

Checking Your Matrix Is Aligned

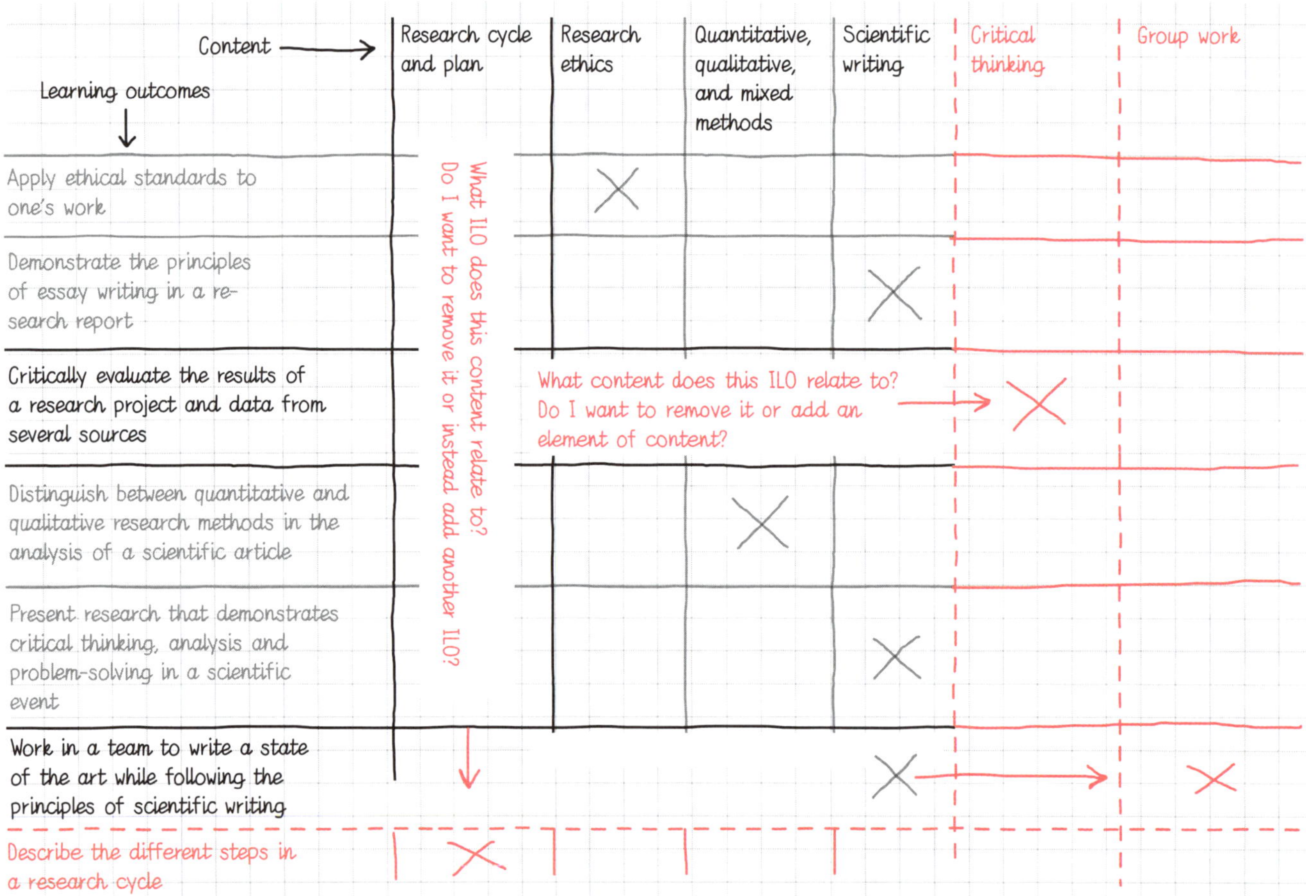

Some Questions When Checking Your Matrix

- Are there any empty rows or columns?
  Do I need to develop content or reword any ILOs?

- Do some ILOs relate to more content than others?
  If yes, is this in line with your teaching priorities?
  Should other content be developed to better match the ILOs as a whole?

- Does some content relate to several ILOs?
  If yes, is this in line with your teaching priorities?
  Are the elements of content and/or the ILOs described too generally?

Things to Look Out For

- Do not choose your content based on what you know, but on what students need to achieve the ILOs.

- Do not overemphasize knowledge in relation to other aspects.

- Do not try to be exhaustive. Instead focus on content that matches your priorities.

An Overview of the Process

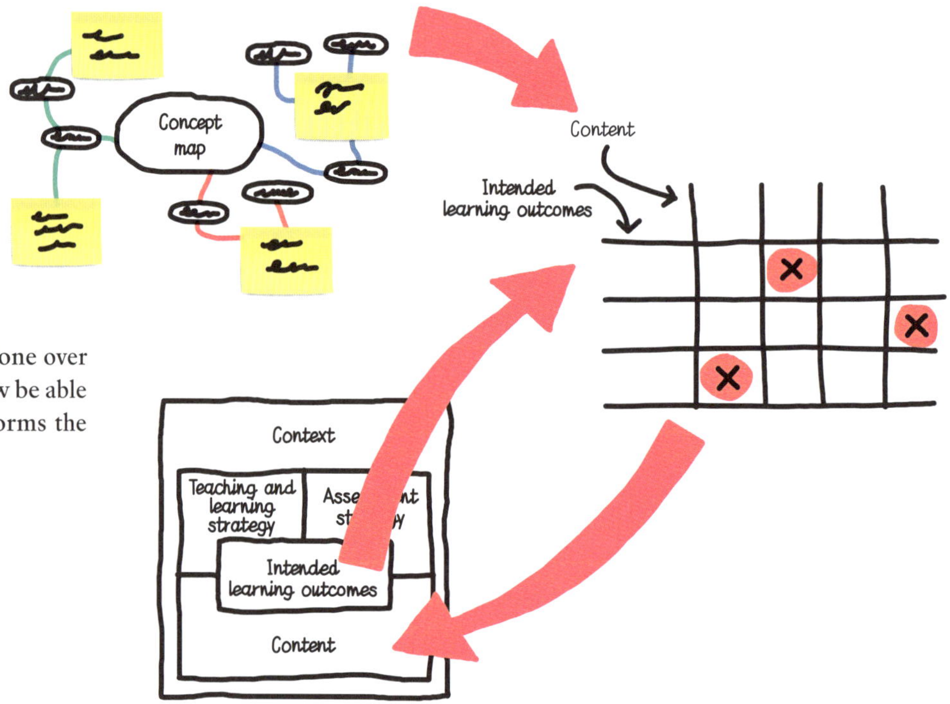

Based on the work you have done over the last few pages, you will now be able to identify the content that forms the backbone of your teaching.

V. Formulating Your Teaching and Learning Strategy

How can I provide the appropriate conditions for my students to achieve the intended learning outcomes?

A Teaching Strategy That Supports Learning

In very general terms, learning can be seen as a change in behavior or understanding. In other words, students will be prompted to do unfamiliar or new things, which may include concrete skills but also cognitive activities, such as carrying out precise calculations.

As this understanding evolves—the other aspect of learning—students will develop a much broader interpretative framework, that is, they will come to see things differently (issue, problems, reality, etc.).

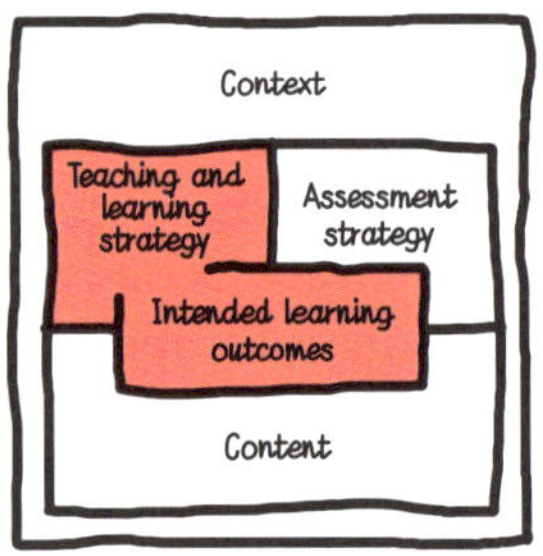

1. Connect the ILOs to your teaching and learning strategy

2. Analyze your teaching and learning strategy

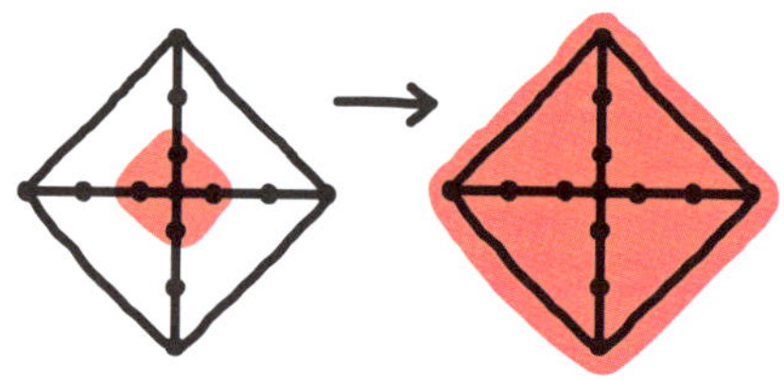

3. Reinforce learning

A Strategy That Combines Activities

Some well-known strategies (e.g., project-based or problem-based learning) and field research combine several activities in order to achieve the ILOs. This means that they relate to different types of learning outcomes. For example, in problem-based learning, activities such as case studies, student or teacher presentations, and debates may be used.

A given activity can relate to different ILOs.

These classifications are provided as a guide and are not definitive. The way in which the activities are organized has an effect on the ILOs. For example, a demonstration, depending on whether it requires the students to observe or reproduce, will have a different effect on the students' skill sets.

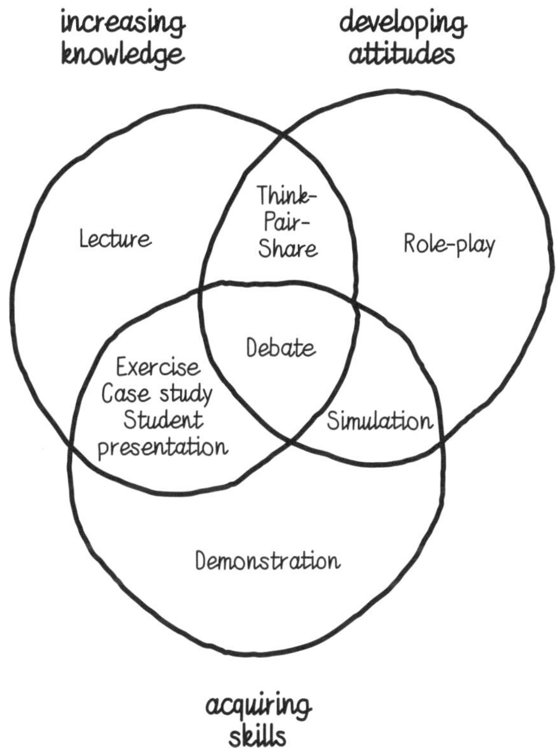

Connecting ILOs to Your Teaching and Learning Strategy

It is important to underline the fact that success in an exam situation does not cover all that learning entails.

The teaching and learning strategy should encompass all kinds of learning activities: in-class or out-of-class, on-line, individual or group. You should distinguish between the teaching format and the learning activities. For example, lectures and seminars are types of formats, but within these formats, various activities can be undertaken, such as presentations, debates, think-pair-share, etc.

One key issue is, of course, the effectiveness of teaching and learning strategies. There is not one perfect strategy nor is there a perfect tool. Everything depends on the intended learning outcome.

Other variables may also influence your choices or may require you to make adjustments, for example, the number of students, the material conditions, the available time, or the teacher's familiarity with some activities.

Intended learning outcomes	Teaching strategy and learning activities (one or several activities for each ILO)	
Apply ethical standards to one's work.	Lecture	Exercise
Demonstrate the principles of essay writing in a research report.	Exercises	
Critically evaluate the results of a research project and data from several sources.	Lecture	Think-Pair-Share
Distinguish between quantitative and qualitative research methods in the analysis of a scientific article.	Lecture	Exercise
Present research that demonstrates critical thinking, analysis, and problem-solving in a scientific event.	Lecture	Field research
Work in a team to write a state of the art while following the principles of scientific writing.	Lecture	Several group activities (writing and presenting a report)
Describe the different steps in a research cycle.	Lecture	

ILOs

To help you describe and analyze your strategy, we suggest you complete the table below. For each ILO, note the activities you have organized or planned that will allow students to achieve the intended learning outcomes.

Intended learning outcomes	Teaching strategy and learning activities (one or several activities for each ILO)

Analyzing Your Teaching and Learning Strategy

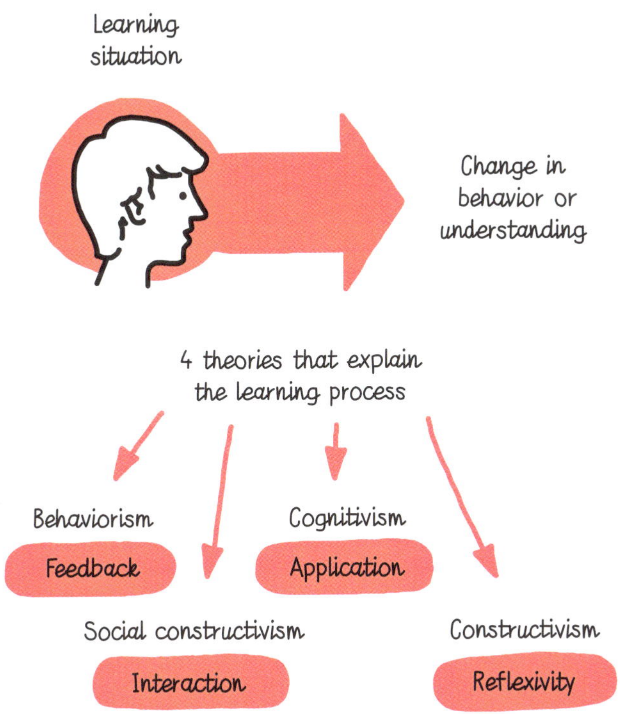

Four Principles for Refining Your Choices

In order to understand how the activities and a strategy can facilitate learning, it is useful to keep in mind the main conditions you are trying to create, as understood from the study of learning theories.

Several authors and research groups have been interested since the early twentieth century in how learning works. There are now many variants of the main theories of education psychology.

Our approach is based on an overarching view of learning, where we have tried to take the best elements from various studies. As such, we haven't chosen one specific theory, but have instead tried to identify the key concepts from these main theories.

Feedback

→ *Behaviorism*

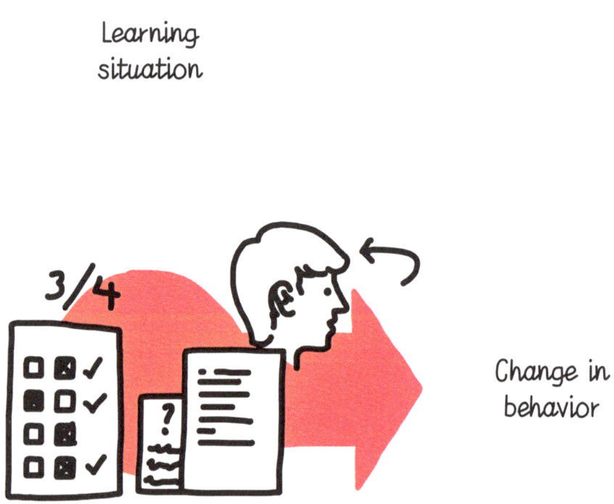

What emerges from this theory is the importance of repeating the information so that students can assimilate it, but also of reinforcing desirable behavior and deterring undesirable behavior through appropriate rewards or consequences to "shape" the students. The idea here is therefore one of *feedback*. So, as instructors, we should reflect on the nature and quality of the feedback we provide to students while they are doing an activity or once they have completed it. This feedback will be useful for improving their learning. It could also be helpful to plan the teaching around specific ILOs, create teaching chunks, and assess expected behavior.

Application

→ *Cognitivism*

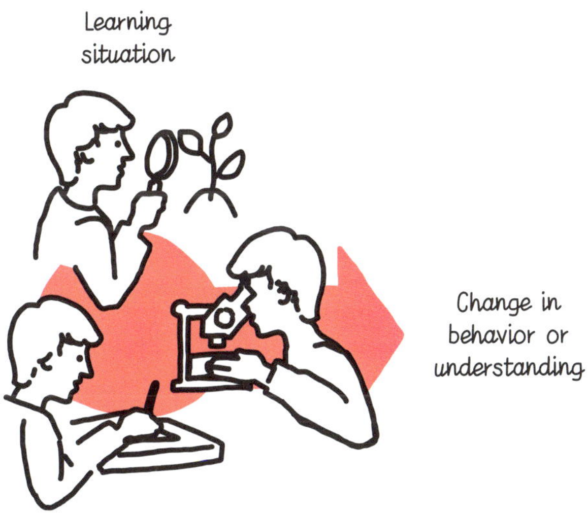

In this theory, the focus is on memorization. Research in cognitive psychology shows that people are more likely to retain information that seems meaningful and useful, the latter aspect being of particular importance to the processing of information. The key notion to retain is that of *application*.

Here the idea is to give students activities that allow them to reuse their knowledge and apply it in various situations.

Furthermore, to facilitate this processing of information, priority should be given to activities or methods that offer students the opportunity to select the information and organize it in their memory (note-taking techniques, use of mind maps, problem-solving activities, etc.).

To reinforce this learning process, students should have the opportunity to apply their knowledge in various situations and understand that their knowledge can be used in other contexts. It is therefore important to provide the appropriate conditions for students to apply the theoretical notions, concepts, etc. they have seen in class and in various situations.

Interaction

→ *Social constructivism*

This theory proposes that students learn through social interaction, by testing their point of view against those of other people. The important element here is *interaction*.

The instructor should organize learning situations in which the students can interact, cooperate, discuss their views, etc. It is on the basis of these exchanges that they will be able to integrate the information.

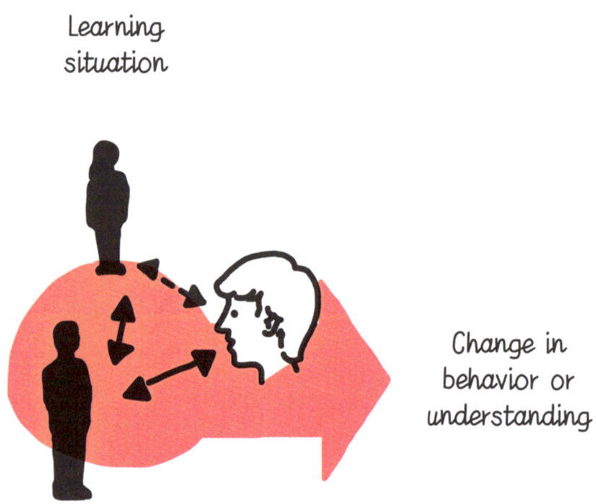

Reflexivity

→ *Constructivism*

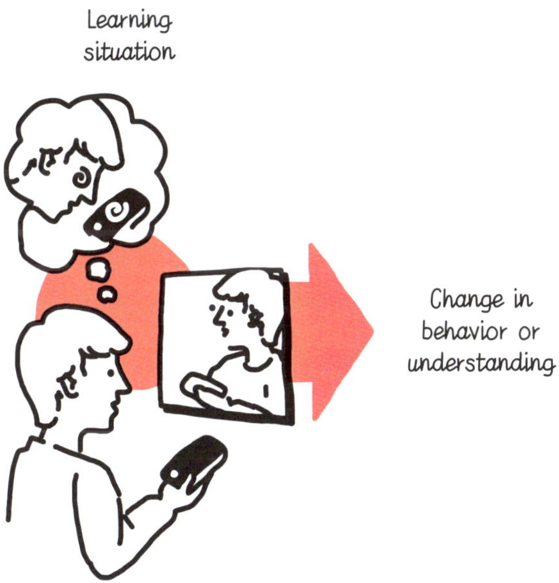

For constructivists, learning occurs as the students actively construct their knowledge. The students are expected to make sense of concepts through analyzing the situation and/or their own experience. The instructor brings knowledge to the class and provides elements to accompany students along their thinking process and help them develop. The key idea here is *reflexivity*. The instructor should propose tools and self-directed learning situations (information search, personal project, etc.) to guide students as they develop their thinking on the basis of these situations and thus to encourage self-learning.

Using these Four Principles to Analyze Your Teaching and Learning Strategy

After analyzing the ILOs, identify whether each teaching and learning activity helps support *Feedback* and repetition, *Application*, *Interaction* and *Reflexivity* (FAIR). As you carry out the analysis, fill out the table below. You can refer to the example on the following page for ideas.

What are your overall observations? Are the various dimensions (FAIR) evenly spread in relation to the type of ILOs or could there be more activities specifically connected to the ILOs? For example, if your ILOs relate to skills, have you allowed sufficient practical activities? Are the four dimensions present relatively equally or are some more present than others? For example, do you tend to place greater emphasis on reflexivity than application? Does the amount of each dimension correspond to your intentions and priorities?

You will have noticed that an activity in itself does not necessarily represent all the different dimensions; this can vary depending on how the activity is organized. For example, at the beginning of a lecture you can provide students with one or a few questions for them to answer at the end.

In this way, and compared to a lecture where you do not ask any questions, reflexivity will be heightened, as will the interactions that follow.

Do your own analysis and use the example on the following page if you need to.

Feedback	Application	Interaction	Reflexivity

Sample analysis of a teaching and learning strategy

Feedback	Application	Interaction	Reflexivity
• The lecture includes feedback on student answers to the questions. • The exercise includes an answer sheet with comments (possibly personalized). • The case study includes an answer sheet with comments (possibly personalized). • Think-Pair-Share, in that students are required to give feedback to the other person in the pair. • Field research, especially during the debrief and/or the comments/marks. • Writing and presenting a report, with comments on the report.	• Lecture, in that concrete examples are provided throughout. • The exercises. • The case study, in that the students can imagine the context or make it their own. • Field research. • Group work requires students to implement the ideas presented in the course.	• The lecture frequently requires students to contribute. • The exercises are carried out by two or more. • The case study is studied as part of a group and/or as part of a discussion with the instructor. • Think-Pair-Share. • Field research is carried out in sub-groups (and depending on the type of coaching the instructor provides). • Group work, depending on how the work is organized.	• The lecture asks open questions, which implies choice. • The case study, in that the conclusions need to be argued. • Think-Pair-Share, especially through comparison and/or the type of discussion during the Share moment. • The field research includes an analysis. • Writing and presenting a report, particularly the analysis and synthesis aspects, contains an element of self-assessment.

Reinforcing Learning

The relationship between the four dimensions seen as particularly helpful for learning can be portrayed in a FAIR diamond (*Feedback*, *Application*, *Interaction*, *Reflexivity*). A teaching profile can be drawn based on the degree to which each dimension is applied (3 is high, 1 is low).

The underlying concept is that to maximize learning you should aim for a high level across the four FAIR dimensions, which means a maximum coverage of the surface of the diamond.

On the basis of the previous analysis, it can be interesting to look at how a higher level of feedback, application, interactivity and reflexivity can be achieved, either by adapting current activities or adding new ones.

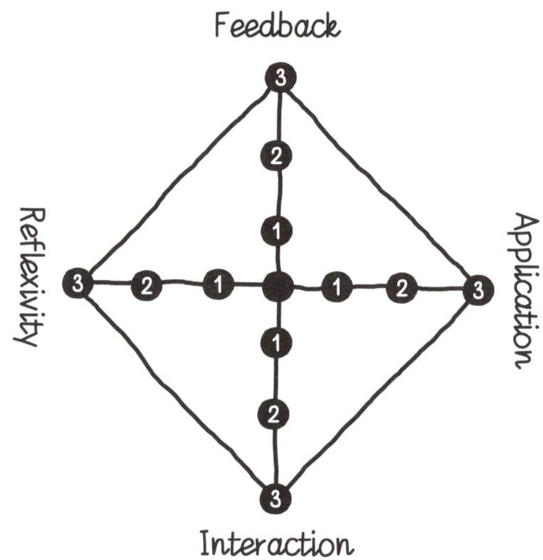

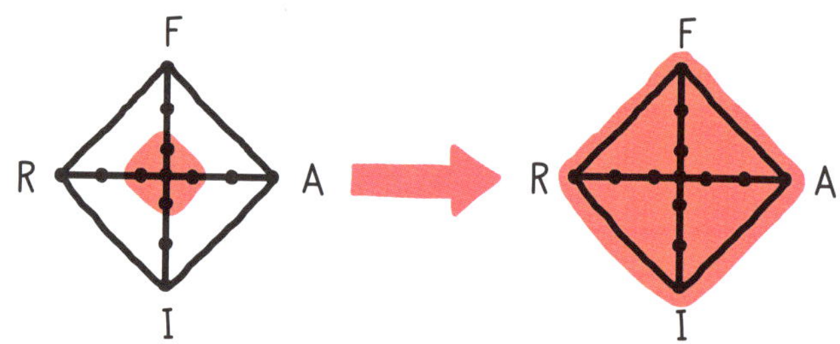

Teaching and Learning Activities

The table below can help us visualize the level of each of these dimensions for a given teaching and learning strategy.

	1	2	3
Feedback	Basically no feedback	Single-source feedback (peer, instructor, or results)	Multiple sources of feedback (peer + instructor + results)
Application	Very few notions used	Certain notions used in a single context	Certain notions used in different contexts
Interaction	Very few interactions	Student/student or instructor/student interactions	Student/student and instructor/student interactions
Reflexivity	Few activities that stimulate reflexivity	Some activities that stimulate reflexivity (activities involving synthesis, comparison, linkage, formalization)	Many activities that stimulate reflexivity (activities involving synthesis, comparison, linkage, formalization)

Examples of application

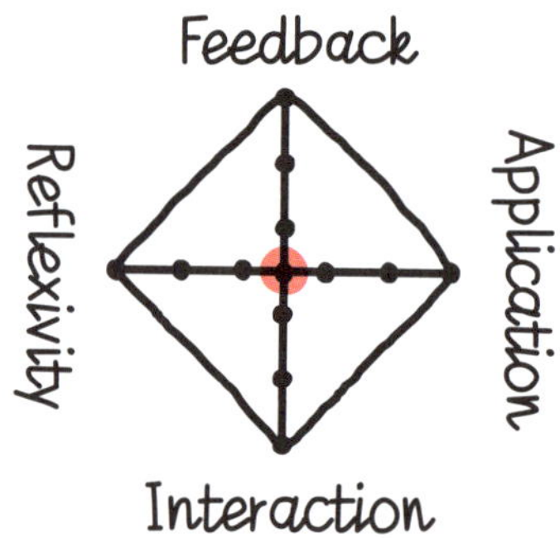

Lecture

In the above diagram, we have chosen to depict a teaching and learning strategy that only includes one teaching activity: a class lecture. Here we can see that the students do not have the opportunity to use the ideas presented in the lecture, there is no interactivity (only the instructor speaks), the students do not receive any feedback (they have to listen and take notes), and there is no activity to encourage their reflexivity.

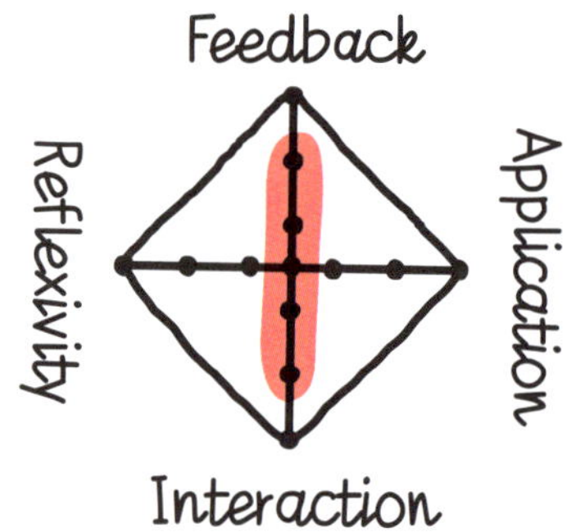

Class lecture + peer discussion

In this second strategy, the instructor has added a discussion activity between students. We can see that although there is more interaction, the students still do not have the opportunity to use the ideas presented in the lecture, and there is no activity to encourage reflexivity.

The presence of interactions (discussion in pairs) gives students the opportunity to receive single-source feedback: each member of the pair can give feedback on what the other said.

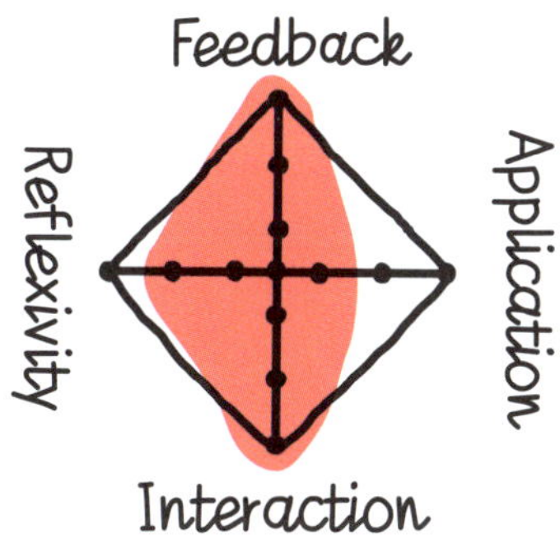

Class lecture + individual question + peer discussion + discussion with the instructor + application of the results of the discussion to the resolution of a case

In this strategy, the instructor gives students a question that they must think about for three minutes before discussing with a peer and comparing answers. Then the instructor asks them to read out their answers in front of the class. Finally, each student must solve a case by using the factors raised in the discussion.

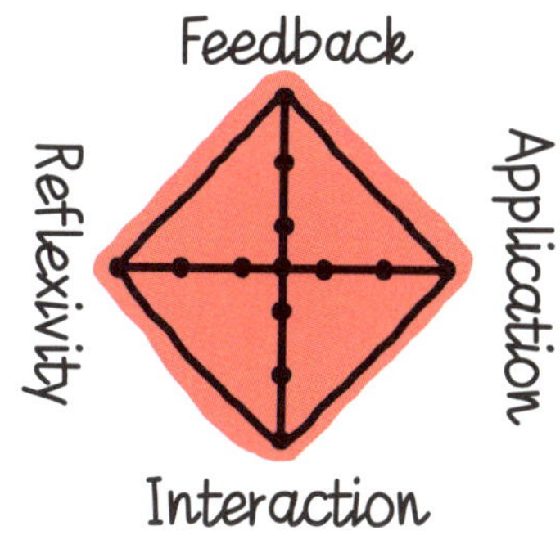

Doing a project

The students do a project that includes a literature review on the project topic, feedback in pairs and from the instructor, and the creation of a logbook documenting how the project develops. The logbook contains a reflective analysis of the learning that occurred over the project and that may be applied to other projects.

The greater the amount of red, the more the teaching is student-focused, thus favoring deep learning.

We can reinforce this learning by changing the exercises or adding an activity, as in the example below and on the following pages.

Demonstrate the principles of essay writing in a research report.

Exercise 1

In its original version, Exercise 1 involves taking essays from the previous year, making them anonymous, and asking students to individually identify the principles of writing, without the instructor having previously presented the rules.

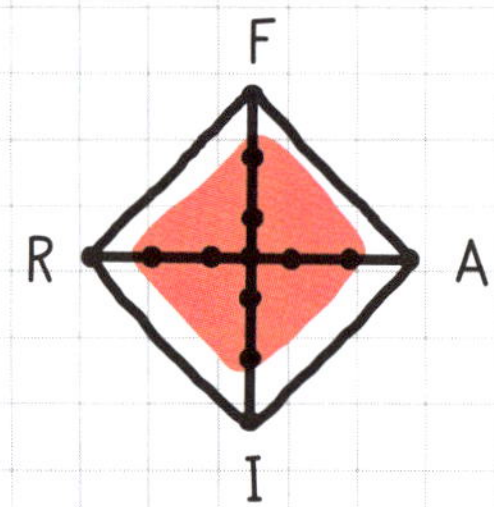

We can see that changing the activity (for example, by asking students to identify the principles) has an impact on several dimensions, in this case on application and reflexivity.

Feedback

Ask students to discuss the principles they identified on their own and then start a class discussion.

Reflexivity

Ask students to identify the use of the principles in two scientific articles.

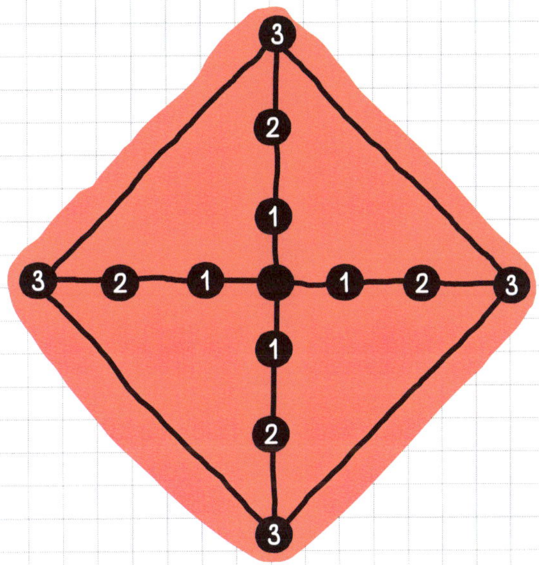

Application

After having given a lecture outlining the rules, ask students to analyze how the principles apply to the original example, then ask them to identify their use in two different scientific articles.

Interaction

Add discussion between peers and instructor.

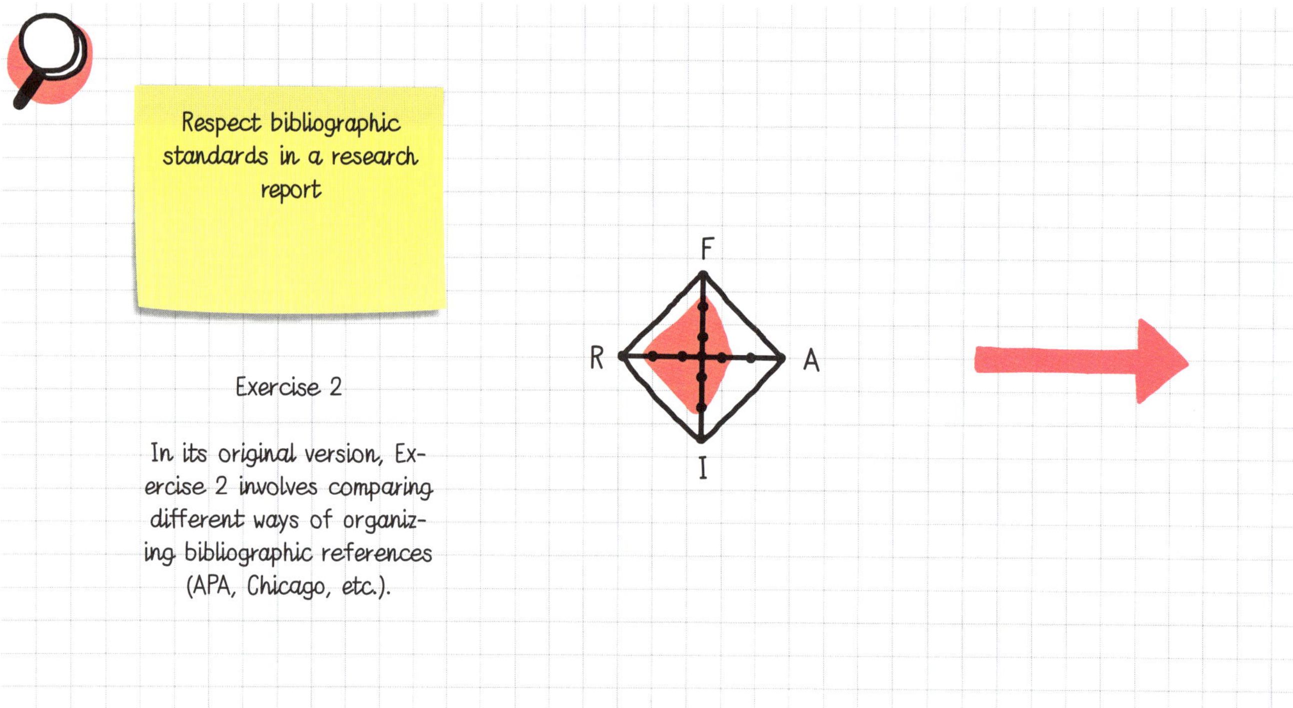

The changes to this activity mostly consist of adding a Think-Pair-Share type approach.

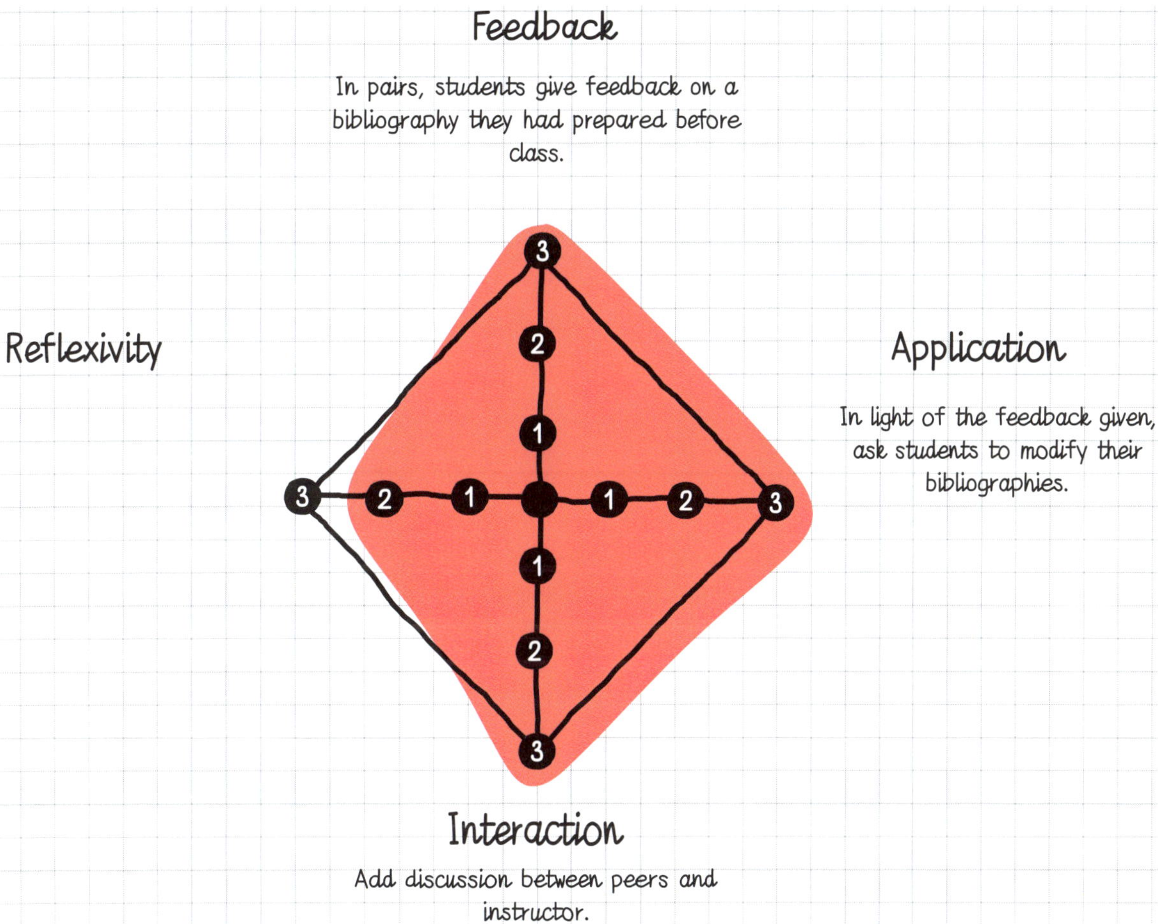
Feedback
In pairs, students give feedback on a bibliography they had prepared before class.
Reflexivity
Application
In light of the feedback given, ask students to modify their bibliographies.
Interaction
Add discussion between peers and instructor.

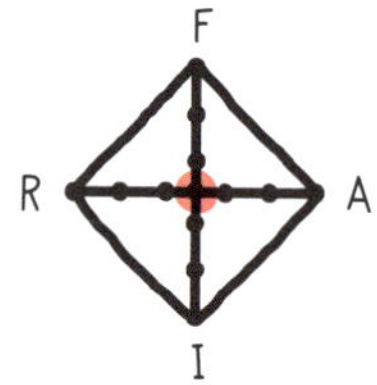

Strategy
Lecture

Description
The instructor presents the course content in a lecture. The students listen to the instructor and take notes.

Teaching intention
Transmit content or information

Conditions for efficacy
Limit length to 20 minutes • Involve the students • Supplement with slides or handouts

Role of the instructor
Present content

Role of the student
Listen • Take notes

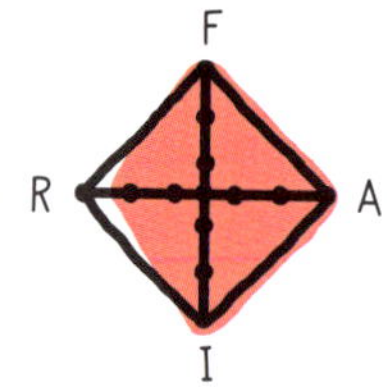

Strategy
Case Study

Description
The instructor presents students with the description of a real situation (or a close to real-life situation) and, usually, asks them to provide solutions based on their prior knowledge.

Teaching intention
Application of knowledge • Learn problem-solving • Contextualize knowledge

Conditions for efficacy
Clear explanation of the objective of the proposed case study • Realism of the case • Clear and detailed description of the situation and people referred to

Role of the instructor
Present the case • Give structure to discussions • Debrief

Role of the student
Study the case • Participate in discussion

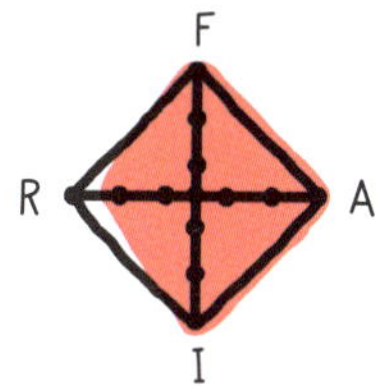

Strategy

Simulation

Description

The instructor presents students with a real or close to real-life situation. The students have to solve the problem by testing several solutions and identifying their effects.

Teaching intention

Application of knowledge • Learning problem-solving • Giving students space to experiment

Conditions for efficacy

Clarify the task objective • Clear description of the situation

Role of the instructor

Present situation • Give structure to the simulation process • Debrief

Role of the student

Test solutions • Observe • Justify results • Debrief

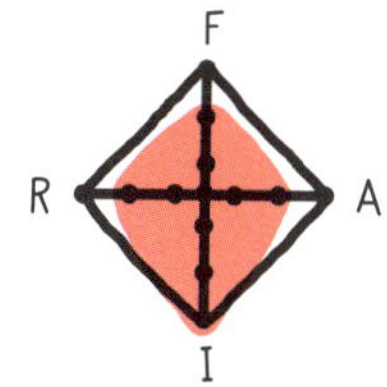

Strategy

Think-Pair-Share

Description

The students reflect individually on a question asked by the instructor. Then the students compare their answers with those of their neighbor or in small groups to come up with a solution that everyone agrees on. The instructor questions the groups of students and writes the answers on the board. This step is followed by a discussion.

Teaching intention

Bring out student knowledge or understanding • Compare points of view • Learn to argue or defend a point of view

Conditions for efficacy

Clear objective • Accurate timing • The topic must create conditions for debate

Role of the instructor

Manage the various stages • Ensure the timing is followed • Give structure to/connect the suggestions that emerge during the class discussion

Role of the student

Participate in the discussion

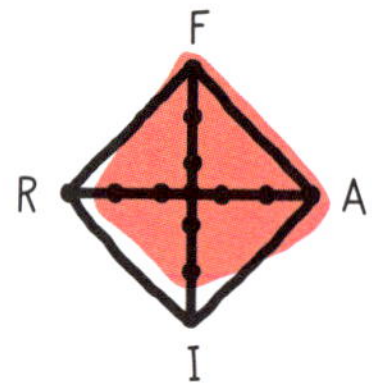

Strategy

Exercise

Description

The students work on their own or in groups, depending on the instructions.

Teaching intention

Put into practice and use theoretical ideas • Automate processes • Allow students to integrate knowledge and assess their learning

Conditions for efficacy

Ensure the level of difficulty is appropriate • Draft clear and specific instructions • Suggest varied situations

Role of the instructor

Design the exercise • Prepare the instructions • Suggest a set of answers • Give feedback • Manage the exercise session

Role of the student

Carry out the exercise • Analyze results based on the feedback

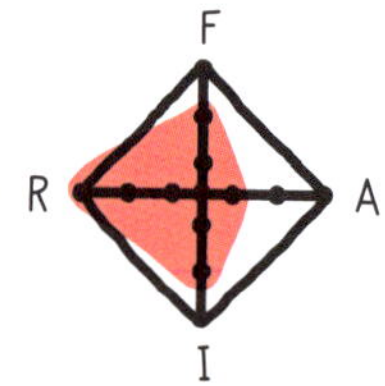

Strategy

Debate

Description

The instructor presents a controversial subject where at least two points of view can be argued. The students are split into groups and must prepare an argument to defend one of the points of view, but also to rebut the opposite team's point of view.

Teaching intention

Learn debating skills • Learn through confrontation of ideas

Conditions for efficacy

Clear rules for the discussion • Capitalize on what was learned in the debate by writing up a final summary (may be individual or class)

Role of the instructor

Organize the debate • Ensure students stick to speaking times • Debrief

Role of the student

Prepare an argument • Participate in the debate • Debrief

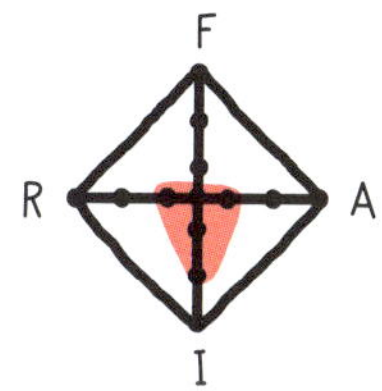

Strategy
Demonstration

Description
The instructor carries out a specific procedure in front of the students, which they must reproduce. In some cases, the demonstration may illustrate a phenomenon, thus making it more concrete for the students.

Teaching intention
Acquire skills

Conditions for efficacy
Limited number, max 20 unless there are video + projection tools and the students don't do the activity • Give a first, slow demonstration (try not to make it look simplistic) • Draw attention to important gestures or moments

Role of the instructor
Carry out the demonstration • Break it down into stages • Identify the most difficult or important stages • Establish a clear learning progression

Role of the student
Observe • Reproduce • Memorize a sequence and principles

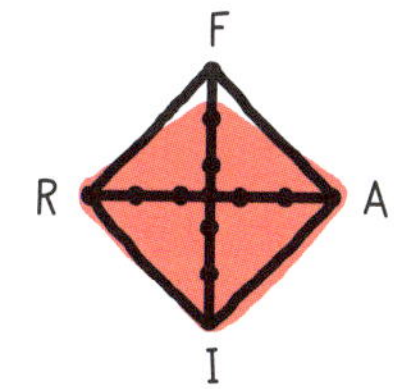

Strategy
Learn through problem-solving

Description
The instructor gives the students a problem to solve. The students are free to research and use any available resources to solve the problem. The students work in a team.

Teaching intention
Problem analysis and solving • Contextualization of content • Learning to use resources • Using students' prior knowledge and resources

Conditions for efficacy
Make sure the problem is realistic • Make resources available • Guide and "calibrate" student work (stages, duration, etc.) • Highlight the problem's key elements

Role of the instructor
Put forward a problem that doesn't have just one solution • Provide support during the various stages • Debrief

Role of the student
Study the problem • Carry out research using the resources • Experiment • Analyze the results • Debrief

Refer back to your ILOs and the activities you have in mind. Firstly, assess your activities according to each of the four dimensions. Next, imagine how you could develop these activities by increasing the emphasis on one or several of these dimensions, as necessary.

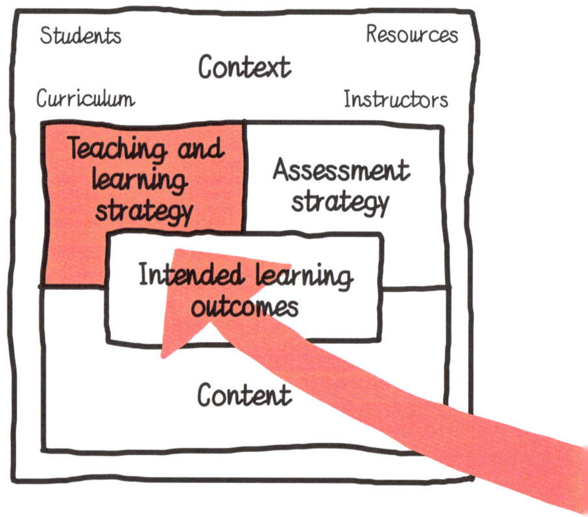

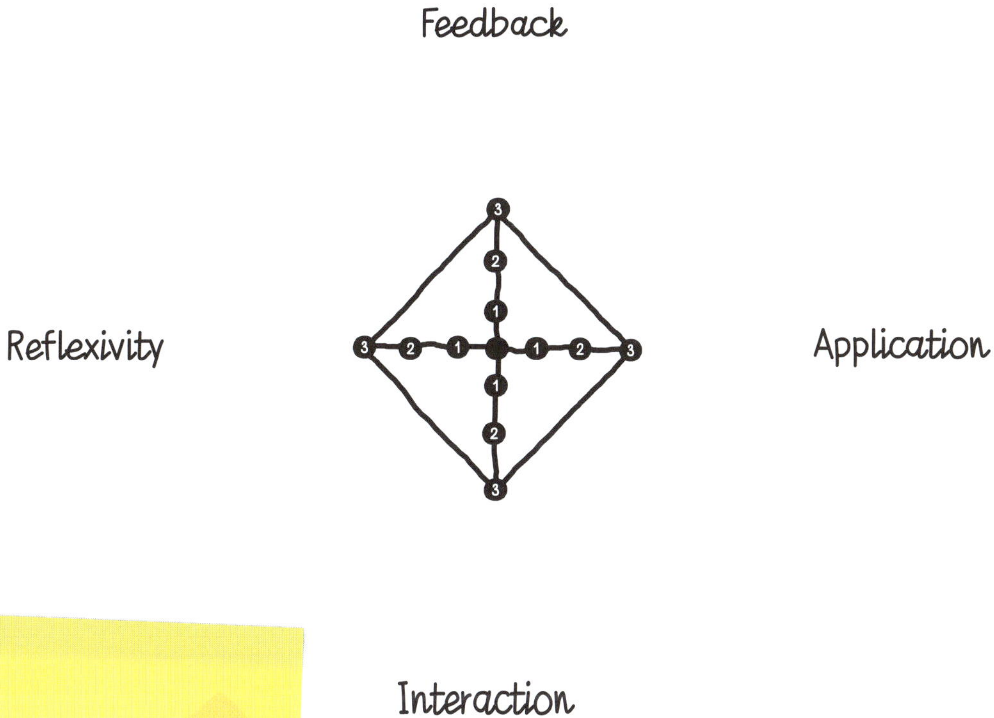
Feedback
Reflexivity
3
2
1
1
2
3
Application
Interaction

VI. Formulating Your Assessment Strategy

How do I check that my students have achieved the intended learning outcomes?

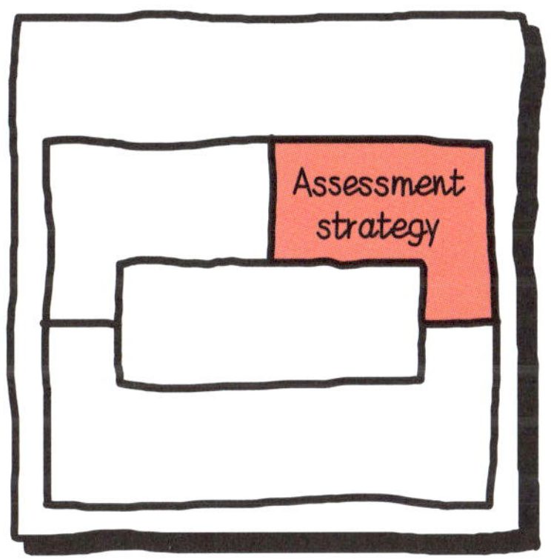

Assessing Is Not the Same as Grading

The assessment of learning involves making a judgment on or evaluating a piece of work submitted by students. Assessment allows you to situate the students' acquired knowledge in relation to the intended learning outcomes. Grading, however, aims to assign a value to the work submitted by students.

In this book, we focus on assessment as a support for student learning and not on aspects related to grading.

Assessment activities do not always involve grading; when accompanied by feedback, they can be seen as a type of formative assessment. Similarly, carrying out an assessment early in the semester can allow you to determine the students' level of knowledge of a given topic. This gives students the opportunity to find out which concepts they have mastered and which they need to focus on more.

Assessment can serve different functions:

Diagnostic assessment

To determine the students' level of knowledge before the course or learning cycle begins

Formative assessment

To manage the learning process, to help students progress

Summative assessment

To certify a certain level of mastery

These various functions are complementary and will allow you to best help students achieve the intended learning outcomes.

Intended learning outcomes describe what you expect students to have integrated once they complete the learning cycle. To help them achieve these outcomes, you can organize regular assessment activities, with a gradual increase in difficulty.

Context is an important consideration when you are choosing the assessment methods to include, particularly regarding the number of students and the time you have available to prepare the different assessment activities, correct them, provide feedback, and so on.

Varying the way in which you carry out assessment will also allow you to make your teaching more inclusive (some students perform better depending on the type of assessment) and reduce assessment bias (of which there are many kinds).

Gradually making the tests more difficult will help your students remain motivated throughout the semester. Previously we described an equation explaining motivation: $M = E \times V$. By carefully managing the increase in difficulty, you can reinforce the "feeling of perceived self-efficacy": the tests will be more accessible, and this feeling will thus be reinforced.

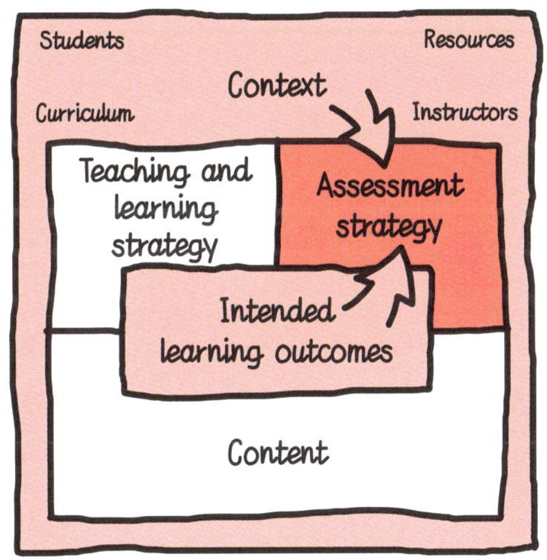

Four Steps for Establishing an Assessment Strategy

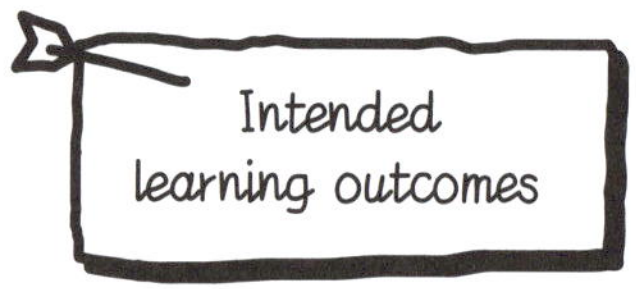

1. Determine which learning outcome needs to be assessed

How do you identify the learning outcome that needs to be assessed?

2. Obtain proof of learning

How do you assess the learning?

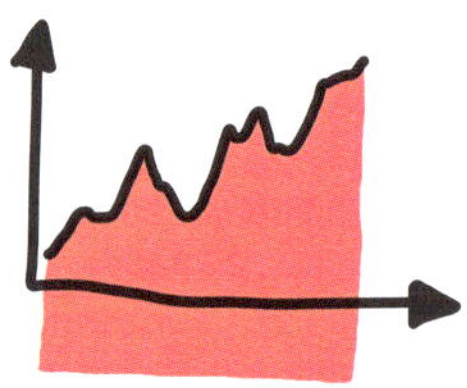

3. Analyze proof of learning

How do you check that the learning was effective?

4. Give feedback on student learning

How do you give feedback to students about their learning?

Determining Which Learning Outcome Needs to Be Assessed

The learning you need to assess is determined by the ILOs. Assessment can focus on the actual result of learning, which corresponds to how well the students achieved the outcome, or on the progress made between two learning stages.

It is also important to reflect on the purpose of the assessment. If it is to evaluate progress, for example, you will need to carry out a diagnostic assessment to establish the students' starting point, followed by a summative assessment to establish the level they have achieved. It can be helpful if you ask yourself the reason behind each learning assessment.

Before deciding which assessment method will be most appropriate for evaluating a certain aspect of knowledge, a skill, or an attitude, you must identify the level of learning. This is where the ILOs come into play, as they will allow you to determine whether you are dealing with surface or deep learning, which in turn will help determine the most appropriate method. You can refer to the action verb used to define the ILOs to help determine the level of learning. The situation in which students demonstrate their learning will also help you to define the context in which the learning experience should take place.

Finally, the elements of content will help you determine the concepts that students must master.

In the below example, the assessment method you choose should allow you to check whether the students can "demonstrate" the principles of essay writing. To ensure constructive alignment, you should make sure the method is compatible with the intended level of learning.

Obtaining Proof of Learning

The assessment methods can be grouped into three main categories: quizzes, oral tests, and deliverables (e.g., a written task, prototype, software, etc.).

To help you determine which assessment method is the most appropriate for obtaining proof of learning that is aligned with your intended learning outcome, refer back to the level of learning you chose and the situation within which students should demonstrate their learning. This will in turn ensure that the assessment has a high degree of "validity"—that is, you are "assessing what you wish to assess."

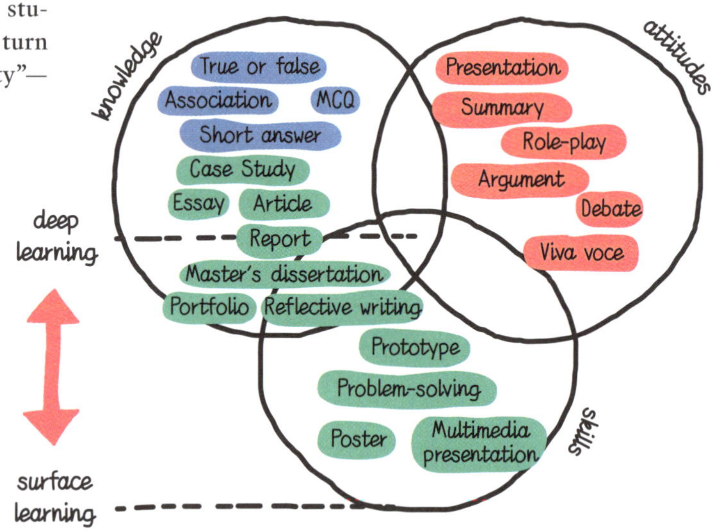

In the below example, the "report" allows the instructor to certify the student's level of mastery at the end of a course, as part of an exam. A quiz at the beginning of the course allows the instructor to verify the students' level of knowledge on the principles for writing an essay, which is useful both for the students (checking what they know about a topic) and the instructor (adjusting the initial classes if necessary or providing students with additional resources). Lastly, various types of assessment methods should be planned throughout the semester to ensure a gradual progression toward the intended learning outcome and to provide feedback for students so they can adjust their learning as necessary.

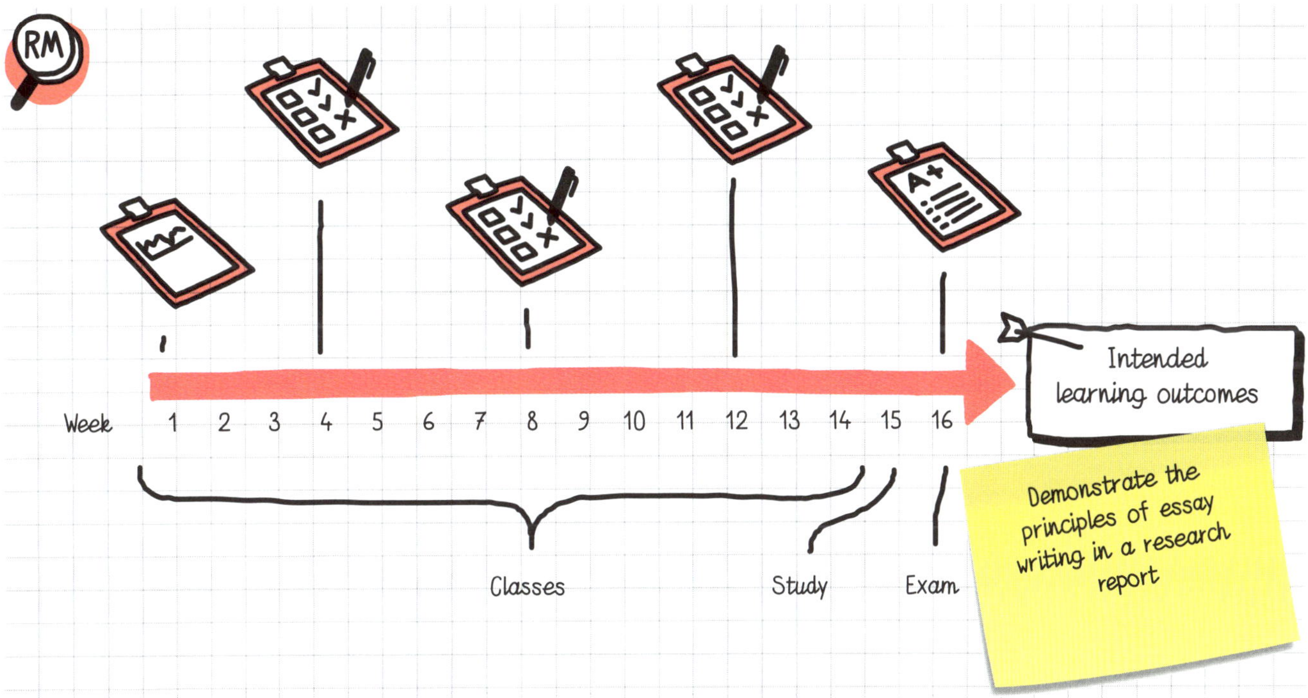

Analyzing Proof of Learning

To analyze proof of learning, you will have to define assessment criteria: what you should assess, what must be learned, acquired, constructed, etc.

The criteria are observable clues that are connected both to the learning outcomes and the chosen assessment method(s). They allow you to gauge, evaluate, and define the quality of the intended learning.

You should have several criteria for assessing whether an ILO has been achieved.

They generally comprise a noun specifying the characteristic or attribute (relevance, coherence, clarity, readability, rigor, impact, etc.) and then the elements of production to which quality can be attributed (concepts, sources used, problem statement, reasoning, spelling, etc.).

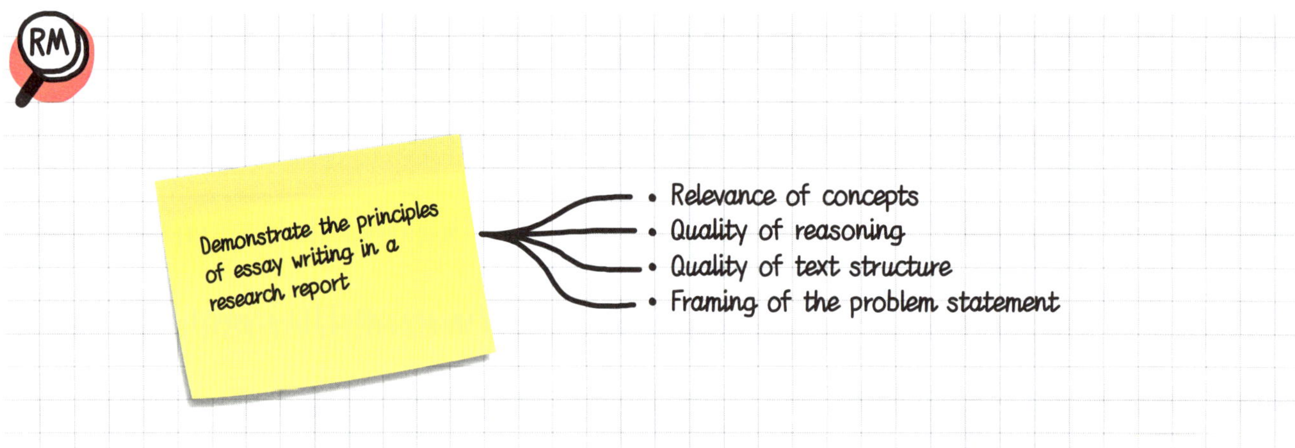

Using Assessment Criteria

Assessment criteria allow you to reduce subjectivity in your assessment and thus ensure greater validity and reliability.

Validity

The validity of an assessment consists in ensuring that you carefully assess what you intend to assess. This means there should be close alignment with the ILOs. By setting your assessment criteria on the basis of each intended learning outcome, you will ensure a high degree of assessment validity.

Reliability

Reliability can be defined as the consistency and stability of the grading result over time and despite having different correctors. Care must be taken to reduce any differences in grading due to different correctors and reduce any assessment bias (well documented in the scientific literature), such as the Pygmalion effect, effects of stereotyping, the Halo effect, etc.

For students

It is useful to share assessment criteria with students, who will then have a clear idea of what is expected of them as proof of learning. It will encourage them along a process of self-assessment, as well as help them to provide mutual feedback and understand their results after an assessment.

For correctors

If several correctors are involved in assessing student learning, having specific criteria helps correctors assess the same thing and thus ensure equal treatment. The use of an assessment rubric for oral presentations and written or other deliverables can further help this process.

The matrix below will allow you to bring together all the information you have about the teaching choices you made and how they affect assessment.

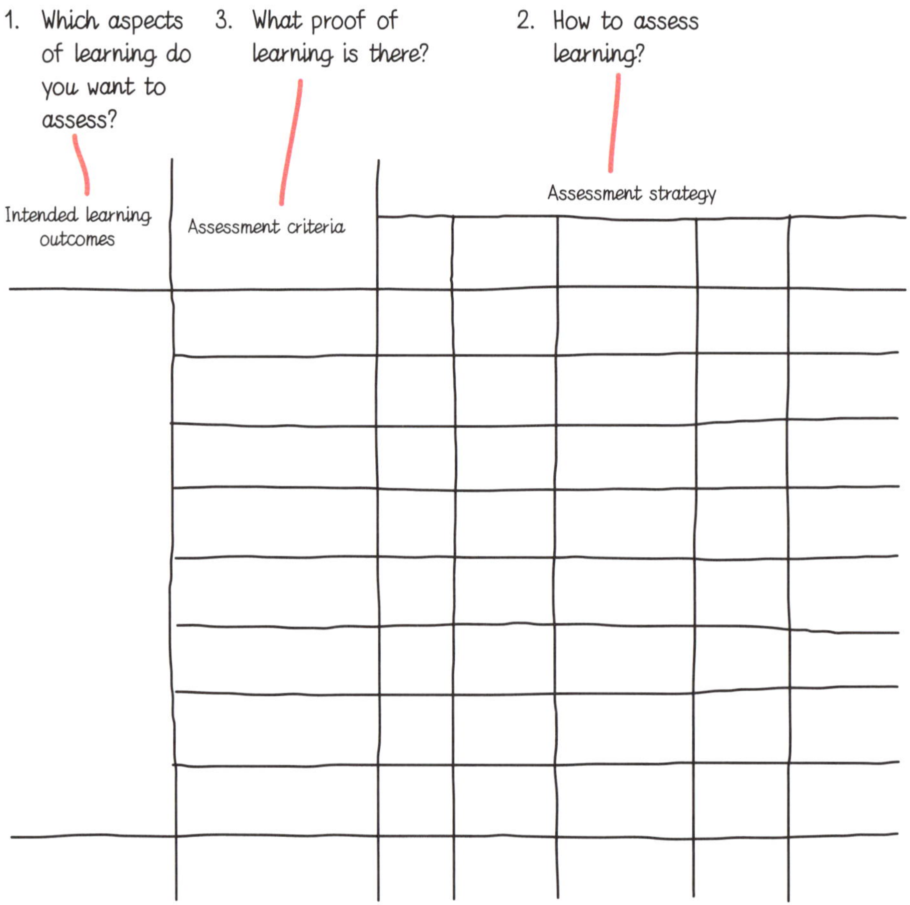

Intended learning outcomes	Assessment criteria	Assessment strategy: Quiz	Mindmap + plan	Problem statement	State of the art	Scientific writing
Demonstrate the principles of essay writing in a research report	Acquisition of principles for essay writing	X	X	X	X	X
	Relevance of concepts		X		X	X
	Coherence of links between concepts		X		X	X
	Hierarchy of concepts		X		X	X
	Relevance of sources				X	X
	Quality of reasoning				X	X
	Quality of text structure		X		X	X
	Framing of the problem statement			X		X

Developing a Criterion-based Assessment Rubric

As part of an oral, written or other assessment task, you may wish to develop a criterion-based rubric. Each assessment criterion is accompanied by an explanation of the expected level of performance.

The number of descriptors may change. In this example, the rubric has three levels of performance: "Needs improvement," "Meets expectations," and "Exceeds expectations." There are no set rules for what to call these performance levels. You could choose a value such as "0, 1, 2, 3, 4" or choose other descriptors such as "Poor," "Fair," "Good," and "Excellent," etc. To make sure the assessment is reliable, it is recommended not to use more than four levels of performance.

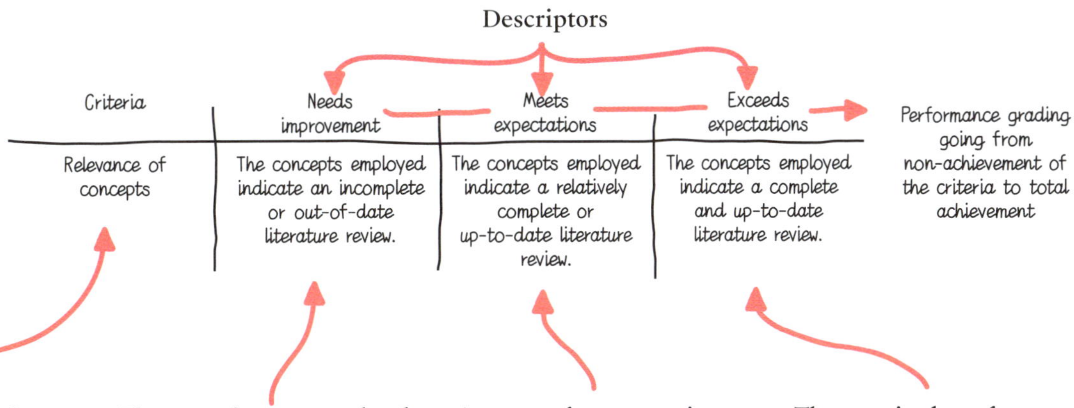

As part of a summative assessment, you may wish to assign a number value to certain criteria so as to increase or decrease their importance in the overall score.

The performance levels should be written in the form of a single, specific sentence. This gives a precise idea of the different levels of performance.

As part of a summative assessment, you may wish to assign a grade to each performance level. By taking into account the weighting and then adding the scores obtained for each criterion, you will come up with an overall grade for the assessment.

The required performance level is generally described first. This means that you can explicitly state the proof of learning.

Demonstrate the principles of essay writing in a research report

Descriptors

Criteria	Needs improvement	Meets expectations	Exceeds expectations
Acquisition of principles for essay writing	The essay does not include a problem statement or has an incomplete introduction or does not clearly develop the ideas.	The essay includes a problem statement, has a clear introduction, and presents the ideas in an unstructured way.	The essay includes a problem statement, has a clear introduction, and presents the ideas in at least two clearly structured parts.
Relevance of concepts	The concepts employed indicate an incomplete or out-of-date literature review.	The concepts employed indicate a relatively complete or up-to-date literature review.	The concepts employed indicate a complete and up-to-date literature review.
Coherence of links between concepts	The concepts employed are not or are only barely related to the subject. The links between them are not clear or sufficiently argued.	The concepts employed are related to the subject. The links between them are relatively clear and well-argued.	The concepts employed are related to the subject. The links between them are obvious and well-argued.
Hierarchy of concepts	The most important concepts are not systematically highlighted or only play a minor role in the reasoning.	The most important concepts are generally highlighted or play a relatively important role in the reasoning.	The most important concepts are highlighted and play an important role in the reasoning.
Relevance of sources	The sources used are not systematically related to the problem statement or do not sufficiently support the reasoning.	The sources used are generally related to the problem statement and support the reasoning in a relatively specific way.	The sources used are related to the problem statement and support the reasoning in a specific way.
Quality of reasoning	The reasoning is not sufficiently clear or is not systematically based on convincing or solid arguments from a scientific point of view.	The reasoning is relatively clear and is by and large based on convincing or solid arguments from a scientific point of view.	The reasoning is clear and is based on convincing or solid arguments from a scientific point of view.

It will take a certain amount of work when developing criterion-based rubrics to ensure that you reduce subjectivity, restrict the bias that is inherent in assessment, and provide feedback to students.

Giving Feedback on Student Learning

To reinforce student learning and ensure that students can achieve the intended learning outcomes, it is important to provide them with regular opportunities to test their knowledge and receive feedback on what they have learned. This feedback should take multiple forms (from the instructor, between peers, detailed correction, grades, etc.). The proportion of practice, testing, and feedback should increase as the course progresses.

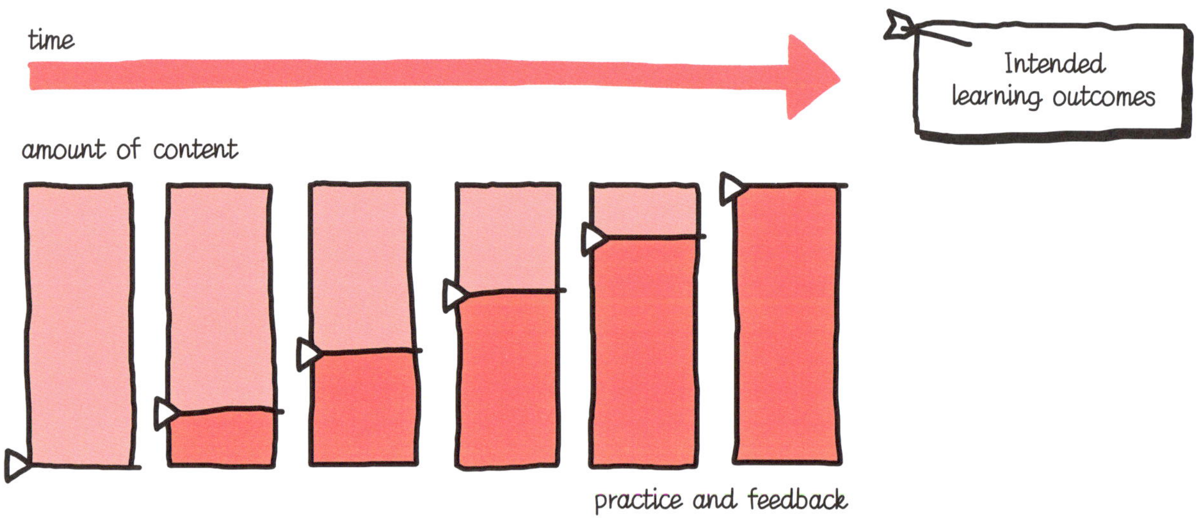

Different Types of Feedback

Feedback from the instructor to the whole class

Feedback among peers

Automatic feedback after a quiz

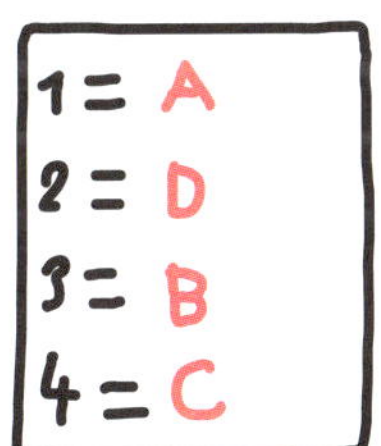

Answer sheet

Grade from a test or exam

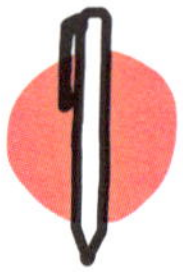

Once you have drafted your learning outcomes and assessment methods, and checked their quality, write them on some sticky notes and place them on your canvas.

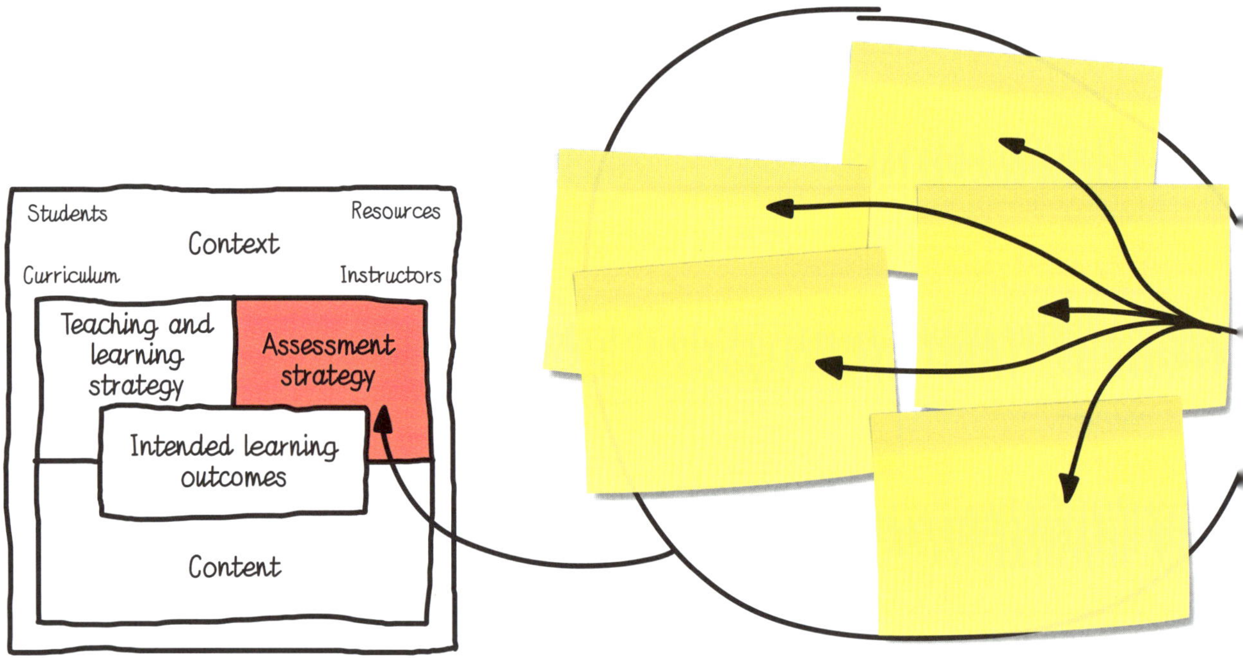

Based on your assessment strategy, plan the time and methods for feedback.

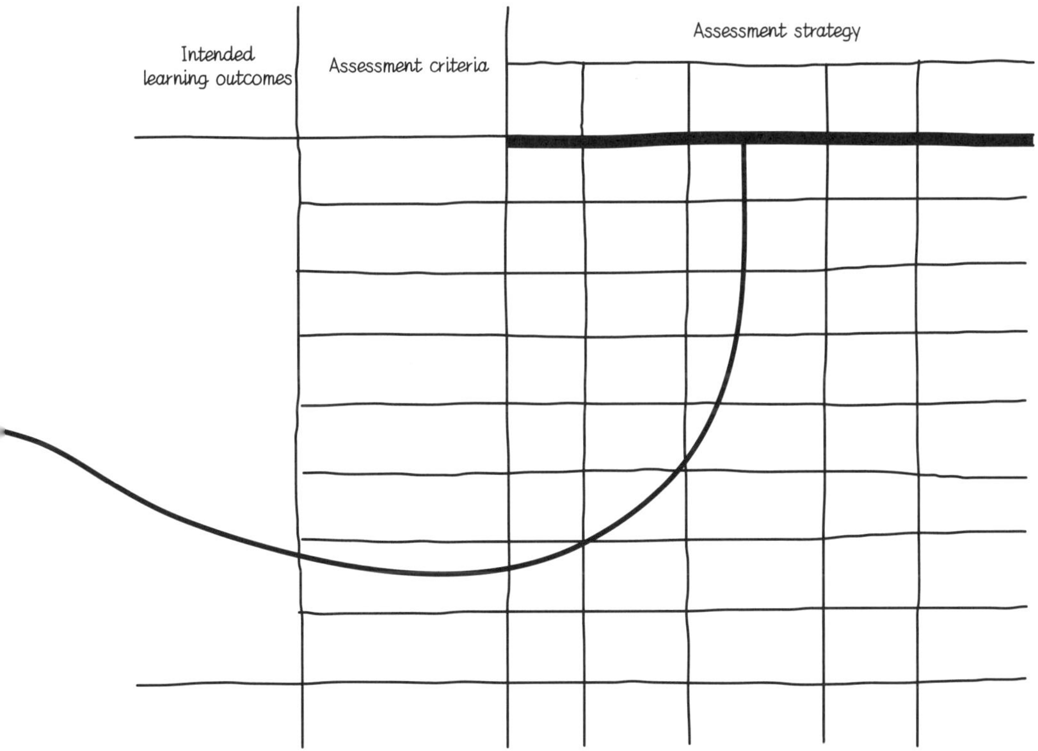

VII. Creating a Scenario for How Your Course Will Proceed

How do you connect the various learning sequences of your course in a linear fashion?

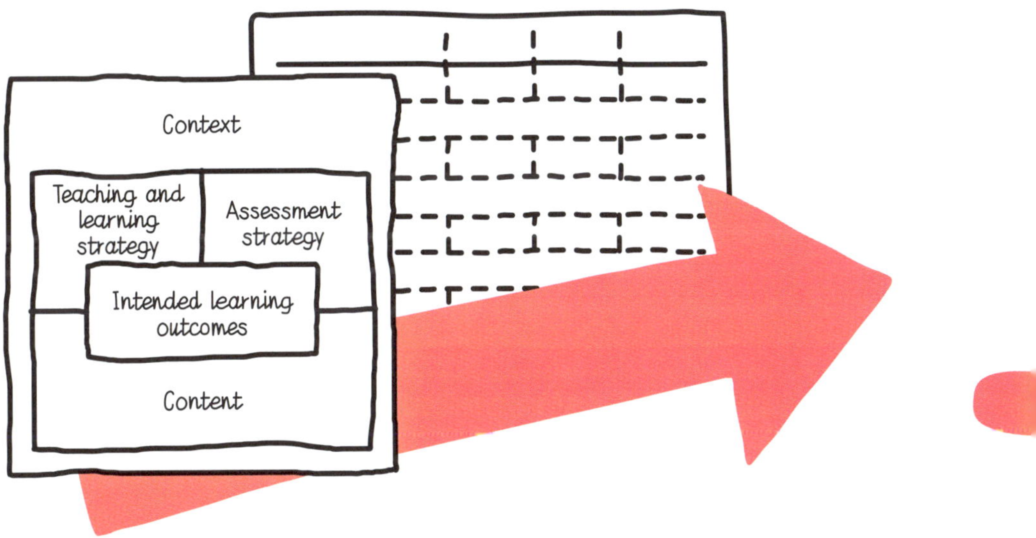

Creating a Teaching Scenario for Your Course

Filling out the constructive alignment canvas is the first step when designing or reviewing your course. Once you have done that, the next step is to consider the temporal dimension and schedule the various activities you have planned. This is what we mean by creating your teaching scenario.

Creating a scenario in this way allows you to imagine how a specific learning sequence will proceed (an hour class, a full semester, etc.). It can also be used to communicate and share your course information with other colleagues, as well as providing a comparative record of different teaching years.

For example, after each class you can use your teaching scenario to note down what worked well and less well. The notes you write after giving a class for the first time can be useful for adapting future iterations.

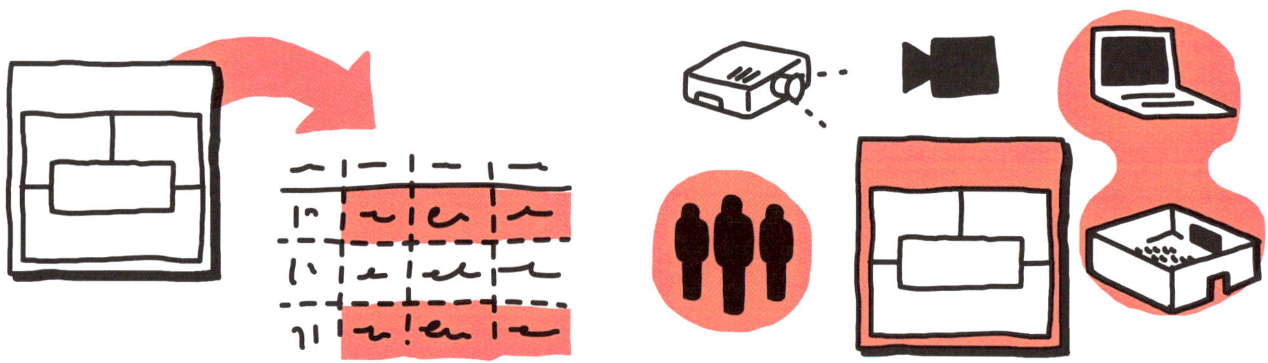

The Teaching Scenario

Developing a teaching scenario allows you to fine-tune your preparation and get an overall perspective of the course, while making the preparation of materials easier. When sharing a course with another instructor, working from a joint document can also help you assign responsibilities.

The columns are determined according to the needs of the instructor(s) but should include all the components from your canvas. After each teaching period, you can update the table with information for future editions.

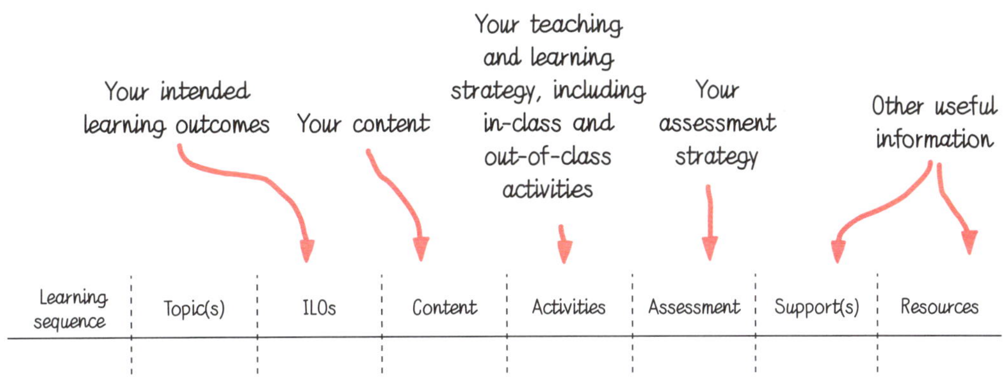

The more interactivity you introduce into your course, the more difficult it becomes to estimate how much time is required. It can be both helpful and reassuring to plan "buffer zones" which allow you to add or remove an activity at the last minute without losing overall course coherence. For example, you could shorten an activity debrief by only outlining the essential points, ask students to carry out an activity in their own time, add an application activity, or further develop an example.

Varying Student Involvement in Class

The below example illustrates differing proportions of student involvement over a one-hour class. Each step relates to a different activity and is associated with a different level of student involvement.

The instructor draws on their own expertise to introduce the subject before eliciting student knowledge. In this instance, the instructor is a content expert.

The instructor assigns sub-groups with a case study / situation to analyze / question to answer. The knowledge and analytical skills of students are elicited here. In this instance, the instructor is a process expert.

Situation debrief. The instructor collects answers from the students and adds further information. The knowledge and analytical skills of both instructor and students are called on here.

The instructor asks students to summarize the discussion. Emphasis here is on giving task instructions and facilitating the discussion, that is, the process.

The instructor gives another summarizing lecture and is once again a content expert.

The instructor starts a class question-and-answer session where students ask questions and other students can answer. In this instance, there is a combination of process expertise (involving students, facilitating the discussion) and content expertise (answering questions).

The instructor concludes the class and announces the topic for the next class, once again becoming a content expert.

Defining Your Own Teaching Scenario

Each course is different, and so is each instructor. It is therefore important to adapt the teaching scenario to the specific nature of your course. Begin with the temporal dimension (for example, class hours, days, or sessions). Arrange your intended learning outcomes and the content you previously defined. List the different types of activities you intend to use in each learning sequence.

Can you fit the course (for example, a one-day class) on just one page? If your course is a semester long, it might be worth drafting a macro teaching scenario (one line per week) as well as a micro scenario (one line per teaching period). Take the time to think about how the in-class and out-of-class activities link together, whether for flipped classrooms, field work or group work.

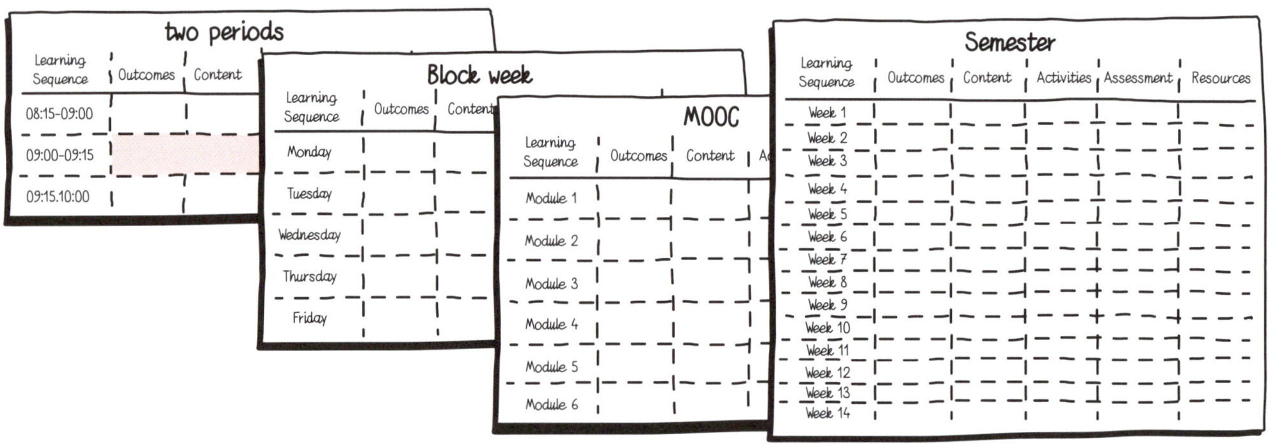

Connecting In-class and Out-of-class Activities

We tend to forget that time spent in class is only one part of the total learning experience. It is therefore important to make sure you connect in-class and out-of-class activities. This could be done by way of flipped classrooms (the students prepare ahead, and time spent in the class focuses more on discussing concepts) or field work (the students collect data in the field, analyze it, and then present it when they return to class). Lastly, make sure that the out-of-class activities include enough time for exam preparation, whether they are in the form of tasks to be handed in (essay, reflective exercise, research report, etc.) or tests (written or oral exam, etc.).

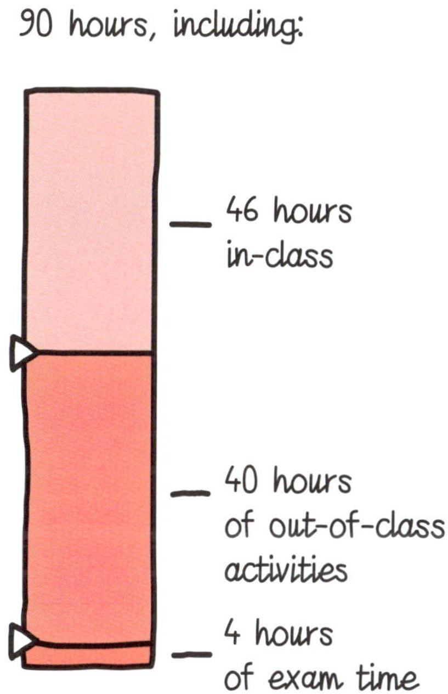

A Sample Canvas for a Semester Class

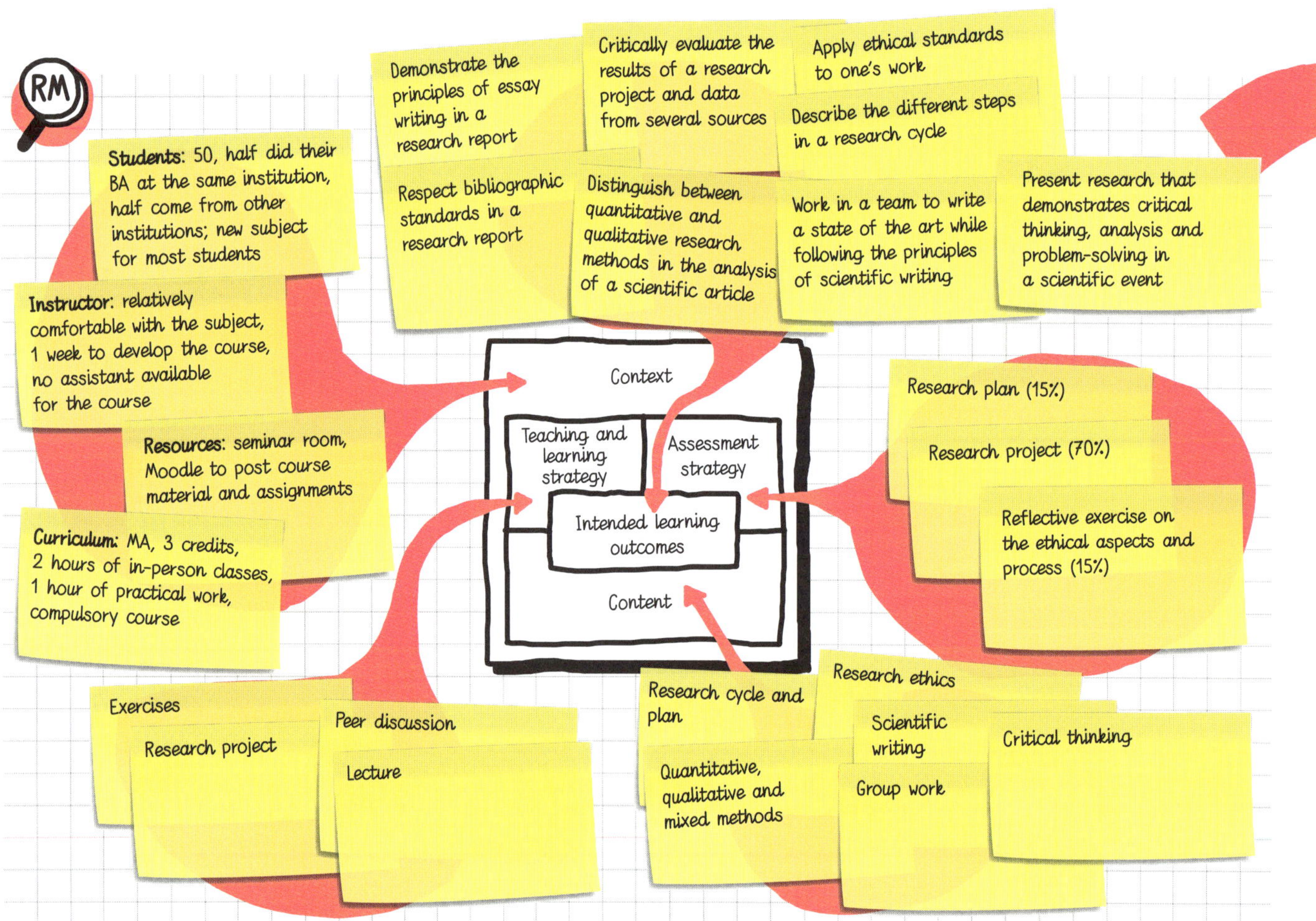

Week	Topic(s)	ILOs	Content	In-class/out-of-class activities		Assessment	Resources
1	Introduction						Powerpoint/Moodle with discussion forum
2	Research cycle I	Describe the different steps in a research cycle	Research cycle and plan	Lecture + exercises			Powerpoint and answer sheet
3	Research cycle II						
4	Ethics	Apply ethical standards to one's work	Research ethics	Lecture + discussion		Research plan (15%)	
5	Scientific writing I	Demonstrate the principles of essay writing in a research report	Writing				Access to scientific databases
6	Critical thinking I	Critically evaluate the results of a research project and data from several sources	Critical thinking	Lecture + exercises			
7	Critical thinking II	Present research that demonstrates critical thinking, analysis and problem-solving in a scientific event					
8	Group work	Work in a team to write a state of the art while following the principles of scientific writing	Group work		Research project	Reflective exercise on ethical aspects and process (15%)	Workspace for groups
9	Methods I	Distinguish between quantitative and qualitative research methods in the analysis of a research article	Quantitative, qualitative and mixed methods	Lecture + exercises			Access to proprietary or open source software
10	Methods II						
11	Methods III						
12	Project workshop	Demonstrate the principles of essay writing in a research report	Group work				
13	Scientific writing II		Writing				
14	Conclusion					Research project (70%)	

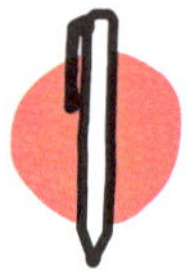

When developing your teaching scenario, refer back to your canvas to ensure constructive alignment and feasibility.

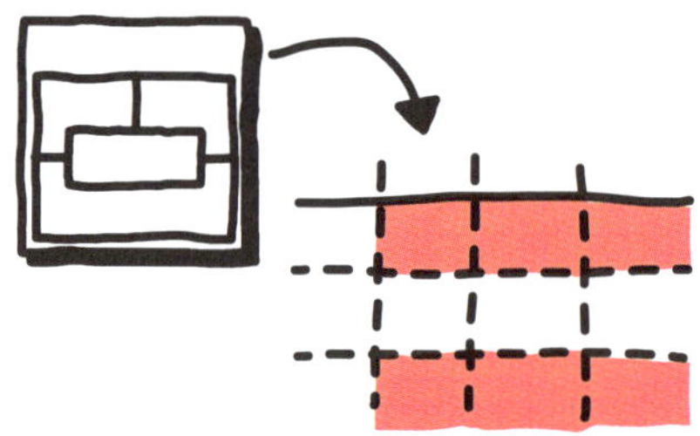

1. **Decide how you want to break down your course: by class hours, by week, by semester, by module.**
2. **Fill out the table that matches your chosen breakdown with the elements from your canvas.**
3. **After you have filled out your macro and micro tables, make sure your scenario is still realistic.**

Organizing Resources for Teaching and Learning Activities

To implement your teaching scenario, you will also need to make sure you have all the necessary resources. These may be human (instructor, assistant, expert, etc.), material (workspaces, prototyping material, etc.), digital (access to online databases, proprietary software, workspaces such as MIRO or Zoom), and/or financial.

Organizing these resources can take more time than you imagine, and you might run into some issues, for example, the heterogeneity of students (whether they have a laptop on which they can work online or a smartphone to vote in class) or excessive set-up costs compared to the expected improvement in learning. Instead, you might vary teaching and learning activities to maintain a high level of student involvement. These two questions might be helpful when reflecting on these issues:

- Will the resources I am planning enable my students to better achieve the intended learning outcomes?
- Do I have access to these resources or the help necessary to provide these resources?

In Summary

Now you have everything you need to provide a realistic and aligned course. All you need to do is carry it out.

From the canvas...

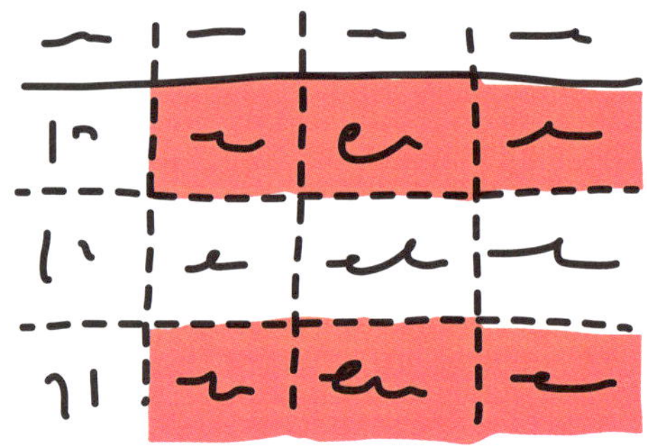

to the scenario...

...to teaching...

...and learning activities.

Develop

This section meets a two-fold objective: on the one hand it will help you improve your course, teaching skills and practice, and on the other hand, it will enable you to bring out the value of the investment you have made in your teaching practice and achievements. The most important aspects here are your reflective approach and your documentation practices. This process of reflection and documentation can be useful when applying for a new position, creating a teaching portfolio, or applying for a teaching award or teaching innovation grant.

Two Stages for Developing Your Course and Your Teaching Skills

This section is made up of two parts. One focuses on assessing and developing a course. It involves taking a reflective approach and drawing on the various components of the constructive alignment canvas we outlined in earlier sections.

The other part takes a broader look at the development of your teaching skills and how to bring out their value. It builds on the result of your reflective approach and also incorporates other tools to support professional development, such as communities of practice and Scholarship of Teaching and Learning (SOTL).

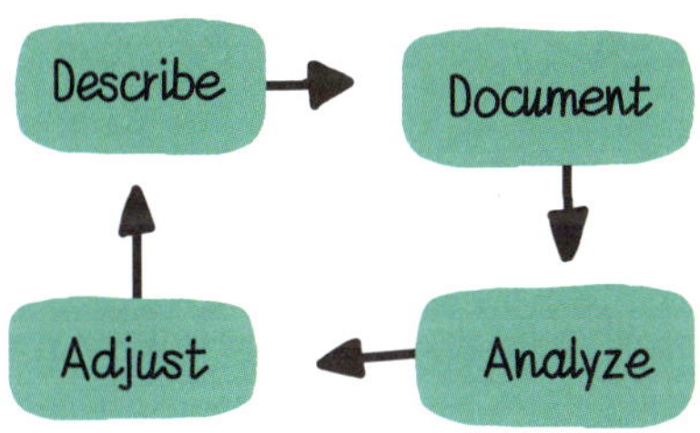

Reflective Practice

Continuing to Develop Your Teaching Skills

If you begin by reading this section, make sure you have already established the intended learning outcomes for your course, because they are the central point upon which your reflective practice will be focused. The "documentation" part of this section will give you an opportunity to detail the various aspects of the course.

Reflective Practice

When it comes to teaching, reflective practice means developing and reinforcing your understanding of teaching on the basis of your experience. It helps you adapt the course to your expectations, student expectations, the institution's expectations, and the teaching context.

By referring to different experiential learning models, we have identified four stages in the reflective process that will allow you to analyze how one of your courses functions and to establish a concrete course of action for developing it and sharing your experience.

This process can apply both to a specific course and to your teaching activities as a whole.

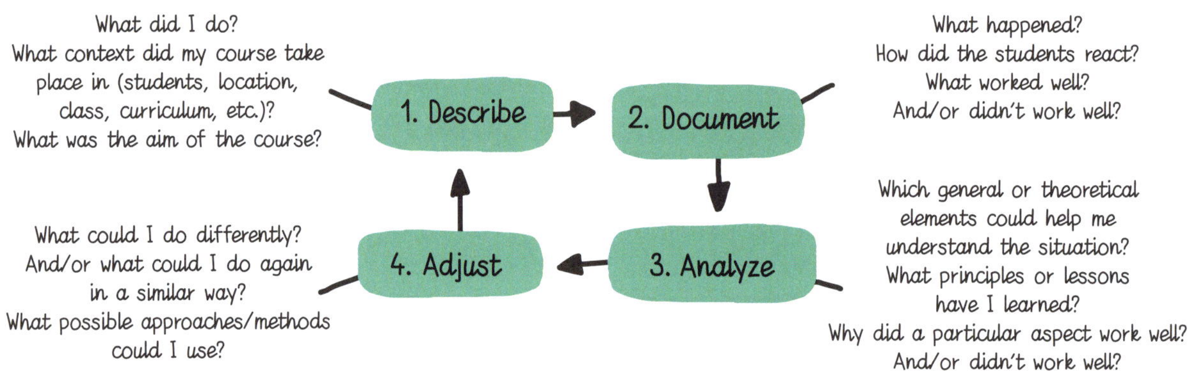

In this book, the process of reflective practice is based on the constructive alignment canvas as illustrated below.

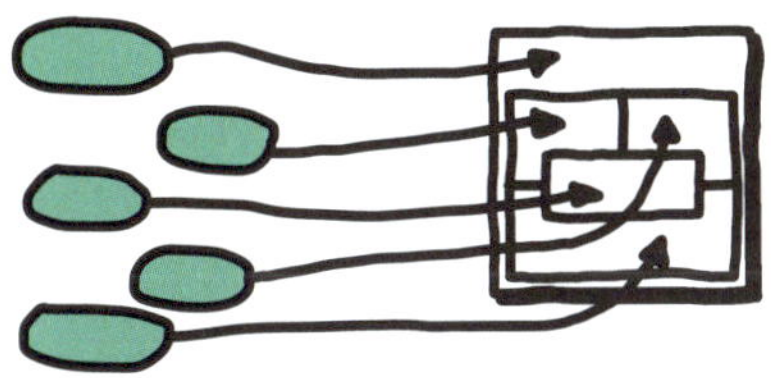

1. Describe

Explain the context and your teaching choices.

2. Document

Identify your sources of information and collect data.

3. Analyze

Identify the main reasons for satisfaction and dissatisfaction.

4. Adjust

Define concrete actions you can take to improve your course.

Describe

The aim of this stage is to describe your course in a relatively precise way. To do that, you can either refer to the canvas you have filled out or use the following questions as prompts.

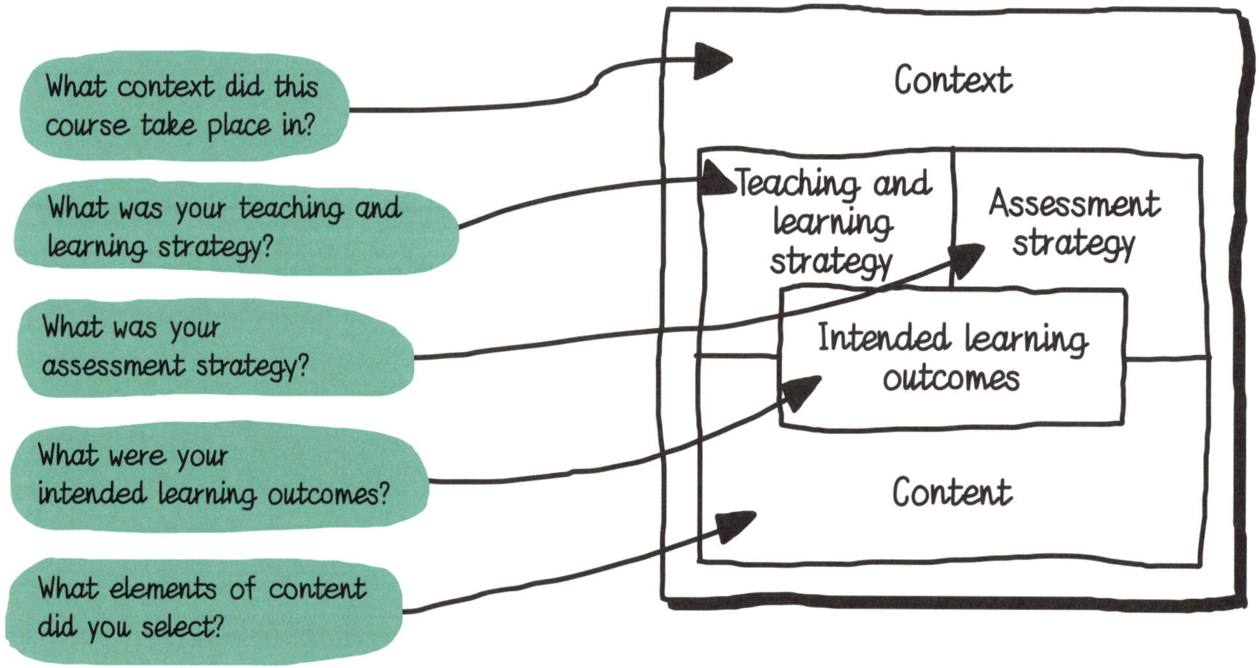

Document

This stage involves collecting information on how your course functions. The information you gather will serve as a basis for analyzing your course. The main sources of information are:

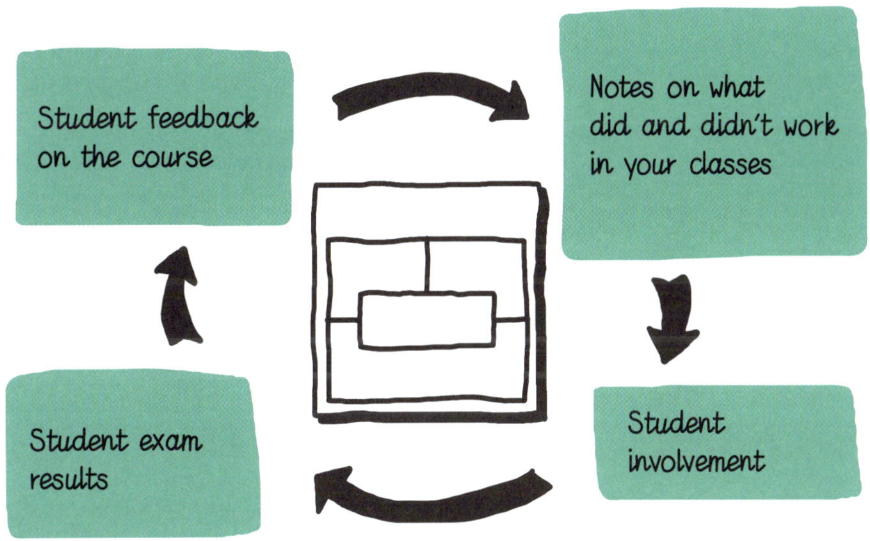

This is not an exhaustive list, and you can add to it with surveys or feedback from alumni, employers, colleagues, a teaching and learning advisor after a class observation, etc.

Analyze

The aim here is to systematically analyze the information and results obtained from the various sources. Research on this issue has highlighted the importance of certain learning variables or dimensions. Without trying to present a full list, we have retained five key dimensions that have emerged from the analysis: the context, the intended learning outcomes, the content, the teaching and learning strategy, and the assessment strategy. We have chosen to draw your attention to specific aspects that emerged from an analysis of student feedback. These aspects are given in the form of questions, and possible courses of action to prevent or correct issues have also been provided.

	Key points How did you...?	**Suggestions for improvement** You could, for example,
 **Context**	Integrate contextual elements into your course?	Make connections between your course content and content from other courses. Examine how contextual elements affect your course.
 **Intended learning outcomes**	Define the intended learning level?	Identify the types of learning outcomes that must be achieved by the students (knowledge, skills, attitudes). Find a balance between feedback, application, reflexivity, and interactivity.
	Clarify the intended learning outcomes?	Clearly explain what the students should know or know how to do by the end of the course. Explain the link between the intended learning outcomes and learning assessment.

Content	Demonstrate the interest or usefulness of the content to the students?	Clarify how the content you presented can be applied and its implications. Show how the content will enable students to achieve the intended learning outcomes.
	Make it easier for students to appropriate the content?	Highlight the most important points and devote more time to them. Use examples and illustrations to aid understanding.
Teaching and learning strategy	Explain and present the course structure to students?	Clearly explain the course outline. Make explicit the connections between the different parts of the course.
	Reiterate the links with other parts of the curriculum?	Explain the specific reasons behind all course activities (seminars, practical work, exercises, etc.). Explain how the various learning activities in the course complement each other.
Assessment strategy	Define the assessment methods?	Present and outline the assessment methods (written or oral exam, project, etc.). Regularly remind students of which assessments are coming up.
	Clarify the relationship between learning outcomes and assessment?	Explain the intended learning outcomes and the criteria for assessment. Explain how various learning activities can help prepare students for assessment.

Analyzing Constructive Alignment

By referring to your constructive alignment canvas, your scenario, and, if you have completed them, the matrices you filled out in the Design section, now you can check that for each learning outcome:

- The teaching and learning strategy allows your students to achieve the ILOs;
- The assessment strategy allows you to verify whether the students have acquired the necessary knowledge, skills and attitudes; and
- The elements of content you include are related to the learning outcomes and support the intended learning.

Make sure that your intended learning outcomes are still realistic, given the teaching context.

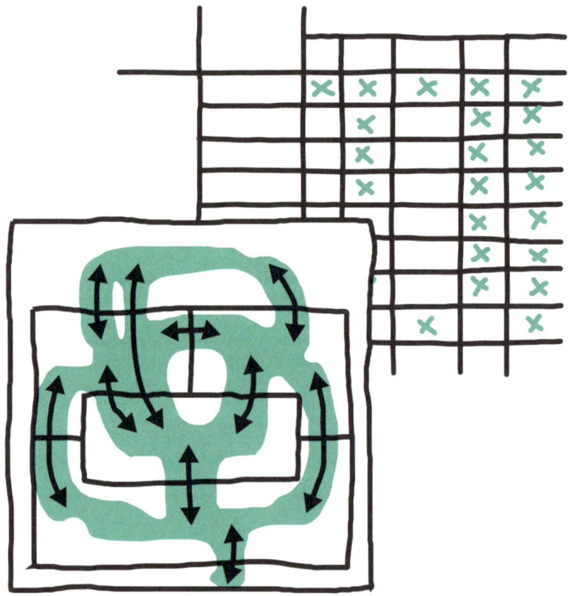

Adjust

The aim of this stage is to make the necessary adjustments to your course. "Given what I know about this situation, what can I do differently or improve from now on? How can I do this?"

The adjustments you plan to make can be written down in the scenario or on the canvas. Communicate these adjustments to your students.

Describe the principal elements of your course for each block.

What worked well? What didn't work so well?

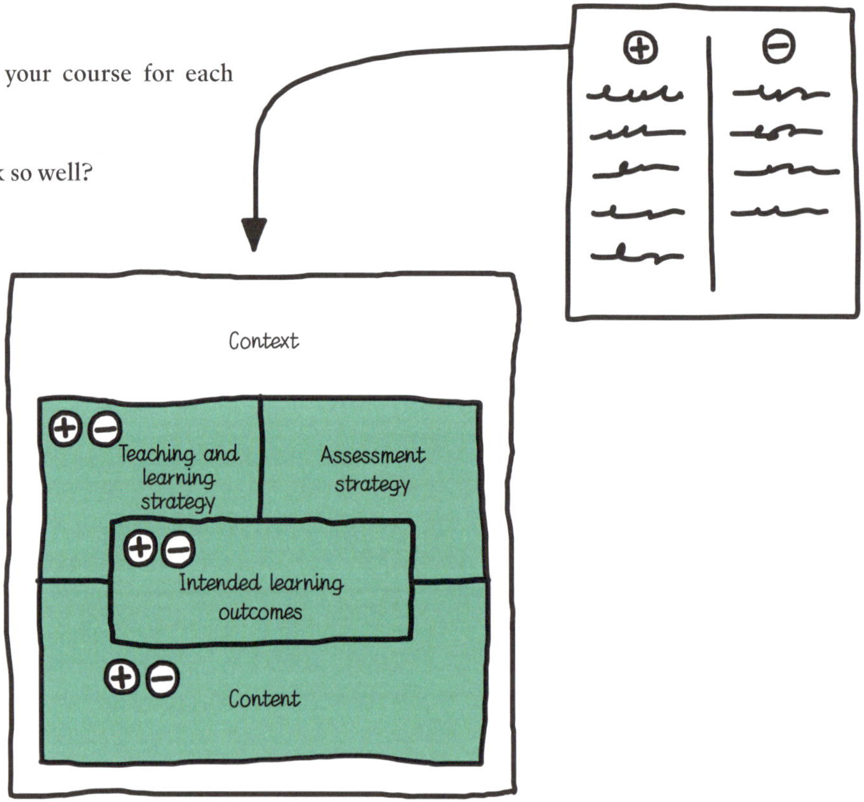

Based on your analysis, what do you think you should do differently? Is there anything you should do more or less of?

Continuing to Develop Your Teaching Skills

Engaging in reflective practice not only allows you to develop your course but also your teaching skills.

The reflective thinking you carry out can be related to models describing how teaching skills are developed. These models generally identify various development stages whose type and description may differ according to the author, but they all emphasize that there are stages in development. One such model, for example, describes the progression from "survival" to "expertise" with "construction of identity" in between. On this basis, we have suggested three development stages and summarized them below. Engaging in reflective practice on the basis of your experience is vital for moving from one stage to the next.

Doing
and acquiring

Understanding
and affirming

Sharing
your experience and contributing to the development of others

Doing

My first class was split into two parts: a course presentation and an introduction to the subject. For the first week, I focused on the subject matter and my credibility. Two 45-minute periods seemed never-ending, so I prepared a lot of material. Student questions about assessment and expected workload, and my answers to these questions disrupted my planned timing. In the second week, I included a "buffer zone" for when student interaction took more time than expected.

What helped me:

Being clear about the intended learning outcomes for each session and for the course as a whole.

Being able to make connections between the previous session and the following one.

Keeping the student/instructor relationship in mind.

Understanding

After a few years, I wanted to adjust my course. This was the ideal opportunity to question some of my choices and diversify my teaching and learning strategy, as well as my assessment strategy. I decided I needed to encourage reflexivity and interaction between students. To achieve this, I put more emphasis on the "project" element in course assessment. Also, each student had to do a reflective exercise to examine their learning and how they managed group work.

What helped me:

Being prepared to develop different teaching scenarios.

Gradually introducing change and determining the effect it had on student learning.

Sharing

Over the years, I had the opportunity to participate in teaching and learning courses offered by the university. Initially, all I did was discuss my teaching practice with my colleagues. Then I began engaging with experts in learning sciences, where we started by talking about teaching scenarios. I also put in place observation protocols and systems that allowed me to measure student learning in my course.

What helped me:

Working with teaching support centers, which allowed me to better understand the field of learning sciences.

Coming up with the teaching scenario for a course right from the beginning and conducting research to evaluate its success.

Doing

When in "survival mode," instructors often focus on mastering the content they must teach. Their aim is to acquire the basic tools to ensure teaching takes place in the right conditions. This might involve, for example, acquiring a method for developing an assessment rubric, facilitating group work, etc. During this phase, instructors focus on increasing their range of teaching tools so they can better adapt their course to the surrounding context.

Some ways of acquiring these tools are to follow general training courses offered by teaching support centers, tap into the various resources offered by these structures, and seek advice from a teaching and learning advisor. Some teaching textbooks designed for higher education instructors also contain information about methods for designing, running, and assessing a course, as well as for communicating with colleagues in a professional environment.

Logbook

A logbook is a collection of ideas, past events, answers to questions, and personal reflections. In it you can note an idea for an activity and describe the context for implementing it, as well as your feelings about how the activity actually went. But it can also involve simply writing notes after reading a book on teaching and learning or attending a conference.

18 19

Attributes of a Logbook

1 Documented

A logbook is a document that may contain written texts, illustrations (constructive alignment canvas, concept map, diagrams, etc.) and/or videos.

2 Dated

The information is dated and presented in chronological order. Dates allow you to see how your ideas have progressed and to understand situations across time.

3 Informality

This writing is intended for you.

4 Flexibility

The document should not force you into a strict framework but allow you to integrate resources of different shapes and forms.

The document could be useful in the future for creating a promotion file, a CV, or for developing a professional development plan.

Understanding

During the phase of identity construction, instructors continue to assert their teaching choices in order to refine their teaching philosophy (understanding of teaching) and concretely put it into action. If the teaching philosophy involves giving students more autonomy in their learning process and guiding them toward deep learning, this may include, for example, developing active approaches and providing more feedback to students.

Teaching support centers generally offer training courses that cover specific teaching approaches (setting up a flipped classroom, teaching by using a problem-solving approach, etc.). They may also provide work placements for improving specific teaching skills. Communities of practice can be set up to discuss with colleagues how to implement certain approaches. And lastly, there are many books focusing on higher education that present a range of teaching methods and their implementation.

During this phase, instructors can share their experiences at teaching days held at their institution or discuss issues in conferences on higher education teaching and learning.

Communities of Practice

A community of practice brings together instructors who wish to discuss and further develop a specific subject (e.g., student group work, technology in teaching, dealing with absenteeism in lectures, etc.), and identify concrete paths of action.

The instructors meet regularly at a given frequency and talk about their practices and reading they have done on the subject. After the meetings, a document containing information about teaching practice is produced and distributed to participants.

Conditions for a Community of Practice to Be Effective:

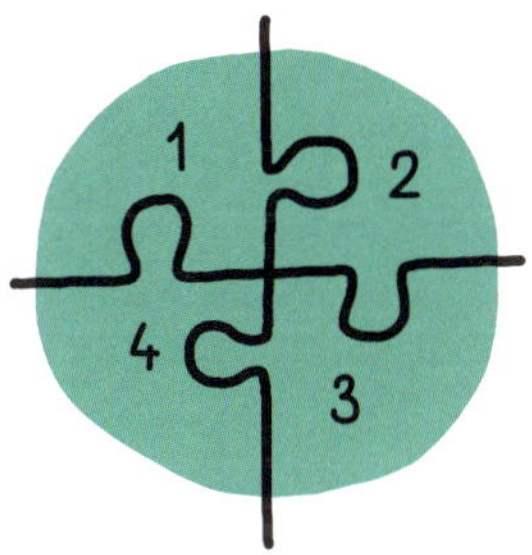

- Active involvement of participants;
- A document containing the subjects discussed and practices to be implemented should be distributed after the meeting;
- Creation of resources describing "good practice" on a given topic;
- Creation of a community identity that clearly reflects the group's field of expertise and activities.

12

Some Questions to Help You Set Up a Community of Practice:

- What subject will it focus on?
- What is the aim of the community (produce teaching resources for colleagues, publish a book, continuing professional development for participants, etc.)?
- Who will the other participants be?
- What roles will the other participants have?
- What documentation (books, guides, videos, examples, etc.) will the participants be able to refer to?
- What activities will be organized?

13

Sharing

In the expert phase, instructors that have developed their teaching skills to a high level of expertise can help other colleagues in their professional development.

They can give courses on teaching approaches they have developed in their classes, produce teaching resources, and lead communities of practice.

Instructors can also carry out research on their own teaching as part of a Scholarship of Teaching & Learning framework. They could then share the results of their research with other colleagues in higher education conferences or within their discipline and/or publish the results in specialist books.

The Scholarship of Teaching & Learning Approach

This approach involves making your own teaching the subject of research in order to improve the quality of both your course and your teaching skills. It is a structured approach comprising 6 clear steps:

26 28

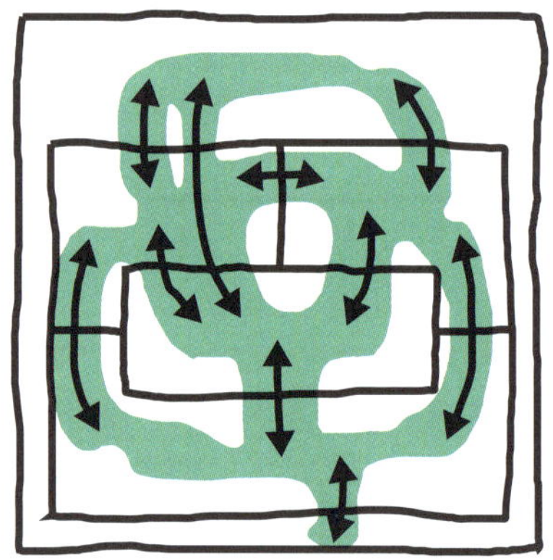

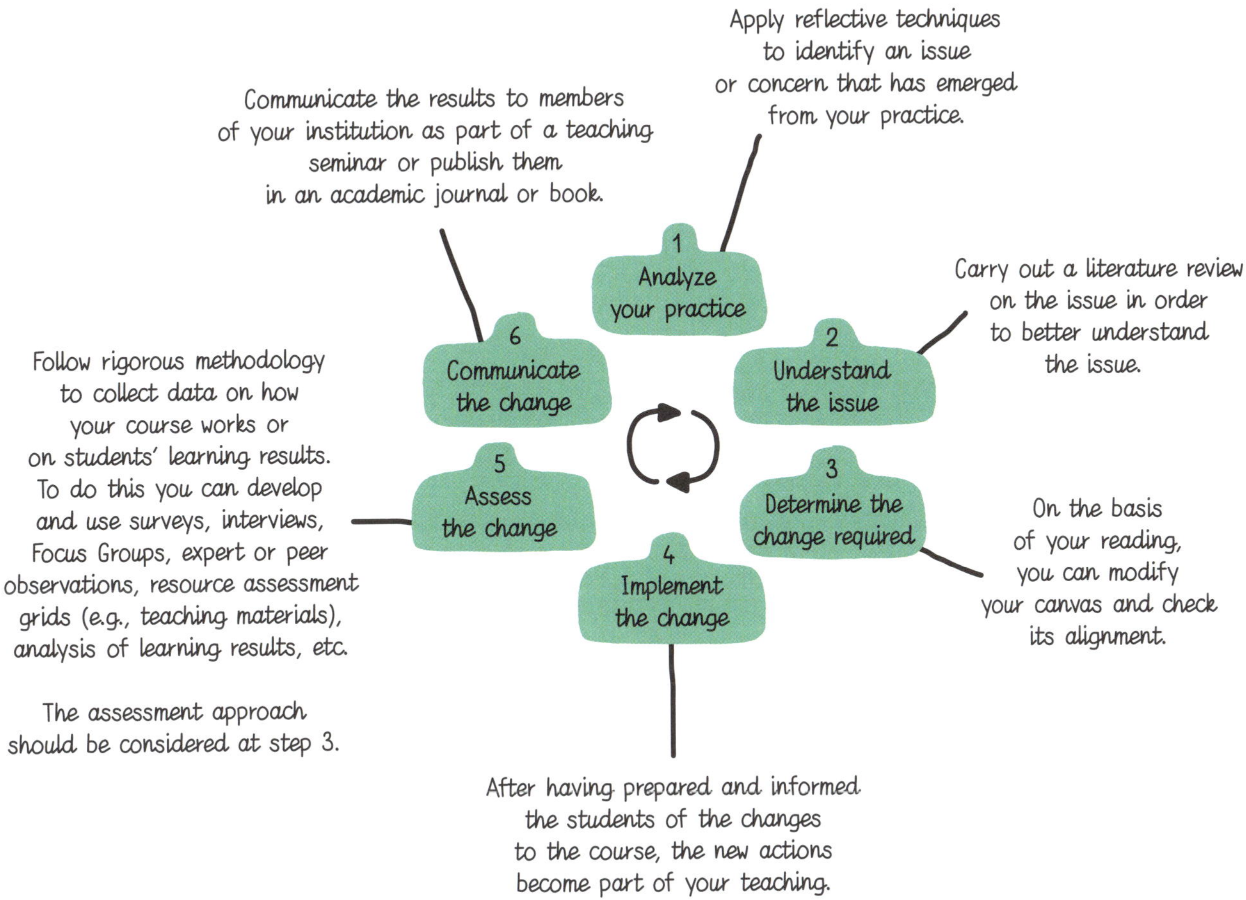
1
Analyze your practice
Apply reflective techniques to identify an issue or concern that has emerged from your practice.
2
Understand the issue
Carry out a literature review on the issue in order to better understand the issue.
3
Determine the change required
On the basis of your reading, you can modify your canvas and check its alignment.
4
Implement the change
After having prepared and informed the students of the changes to the course, the new actions become part of your teaching.
5
Assess the change
Follow rigorous methodology to collect data on how your course works or on students' learning results. To do this you can develop and use surveys, interviews, Focus Groups, expert or peer observations, resource assessment grids (e.g., teaching materials), analysis of learning results, etc.
The assessment approach should be considered at step 3.
6
Communicate the change
Communicate the results to members of your institution as part of a teaching seminar or publish them in an academic journal or book.

As a Conclusion

After this process of analysis and reflection, you will probably want to make adjustments to your course and continue to develop and bring out the value in your teaching skills. These are often stimulating projects but can require a substantial investment in time and energy. To ensure that your motivation remains high, we suggest that you:

- Start with small steps and proceed gradually. For example, in one year you might revise one or two class sessions or other teaching segments without necessarily changing everything in one go. In this way you will steadily develop your teaching practice to ensure it corresponds with your intentions.
- Seek advice and help from teaching and learning support centers. They can give you another perspective on your teaching practice and can suggest avenues for analysis and action, as well as provide multiple resources. Talking about your experiences with colleagues is also an excellent way of reinforcing your reflective practice and coming up with new ideas.
- Remember that professional development is a "work in progress" and that some experiences may be less successful than others. Not all attempts work the first time. When this happens, you should continue your process of analysis and keep trying new approaches, while using the information in this book as a guide.

In any case, remember that there is not just one correct way to do things. There is no miracle solution that guarantees success. The aim of this book is on no account to defend a normative approach or a single "right" way of teaching. Instead, we have endeavored to provide you with reference points to help direct your thinking and tools to help you take action, while emphasizing the importance of aligning your choices and applying a systemic view to all the dimensions that teaching involves.

Bibliography

Teaching Approaches

1 Cooper, P. A. (1993). Paradigm Shifts in Designed Instruction: From Behaviorism to Cognitivism to Constructivism. *Educational Technology*, 33(5), 12–19. http://www.jstor.org/stable/44428049

2 Ertmer, P. A., & Newby, T. J. (2013). Behaviorism, cognitivism, constructivism: Comparing critical features from an instructional design perspective. *Performance improvement quarterly*, 26(2), 43-71.

3 Hativa, N. (2001). *Teaching for effective learning in higher education*. Springer Science & Business Media.

Constructive Alignment

4 Biggs, J. (1987). *Student Approaches to Learning and Studying*. Hawthorn: Australian Council for Educational Research.

5 Biggs, J., & Tang, C. (2011). *Teaching for quality learning at university*. London: The Society for Research into Higher Education & Open University Press.

6 Larkin, H., & Richardson, B. (2013). Creating high challenge/high support academic environments through constructive alignment: Student outcomes. *Teaching in higher education*, 18(2), 192-204.

7 Leclercq, D. (1995). *Conception d'interventions et construction de produits pour la formation*. Liège: Éditions de l'Université de Liège.

8 Sylvestre, E., & Maitre, J.-P. (2018). Cohérence pédagogique et approche-programme : les évolutions de la pédagogie universitaire en formation d'orthophonie-logopédie. *Rééducation orthophonique*, 55(276), 15-30.

9 Tyler, R. W. (1949). *Basic principles of curriculum and instruction*. Chicago: The University Of Chicago Press.

Concept Map

10 Novak, J. D. (1998). *Learning, creating, and using knowledge: Concept maps as facilitative tools in schools and corporations*. Mahwah, NJ: Lawrence Erlbaum.

11 Novak, J. D. & Cañas, A. J. (2006). *The theory underlying concept maps and how to construct them*. Florida Institute for Human Machine Cognition (IHMC). https://cmap.ihmc.us/docs/theory-of-concept-maps

Communities of Practice

12 Daele A., & Dumont A. (2015). Participer à une communauté de pratique pour se développer. In D. Berthiaume & N. Rege Colet (eds.) *La pédagogie de l'enseignement supérieur: repères théoriques et applications pratiques*, Tome 2: se développer au titre d'enseignant (p. 185-202). Bern: Peter Lang.

13 Wenger, E. (1998). Communities of practice: Learning as a social system. *Systems thinker*, 9(5), 2-3.

Teaching Contract

14 O'Brien, J. G., Millis, B. J., & Cohen, M. W. (2009). *The course syllabus: A learning-centered approach*. John Wiley & Sons.

15 Brousseau, G. (2011). *La théorie des situations didactiques en mathématiques* (No. 5-1, p. 101-104). Presses universitaires de Rennes.

16 Houssaye, J. (2014). *Le triangle pédagogique: les différentes facettes de la pédagogie*. Paris: ESF.

17 Terrisse, A. (2001). *Contrat pédagogique et contrat didactique*. In P. Jonnaert & S. Laurin (Eds.), Les didactiques des disciplines: Un débat contemporain (p. 99). Québec: PUQ.

Logbook

18 Shepherd, M. (2006). Using a learning journal to improve professional practice: A journey of personal and professional self-discovery. *Reflective practice*, 7(3), 333-348.

19 Stevens, D. D., & Cooper, J. E. (2020). *Journal keeping: How to use reflective writing for learning, teaching, professional insight and positive change*. Stylus Publishing, LLC.

Motivation

20 Deci, E. L., & Ryan, R. M. (1987). The support of autonomy and the control of behavior. *Journal of personality and social psychology*, 53(6), 1024.

21 Pajares, F., & Schunk, D. H. (2002). Self and self-belief in psychology and education: A historical perspective. In *Improving academic achievement* (p. 3-21). Academic Press.

22 Woolfolk, A. (2018). *Educational Psychology* (14th Edition). Pearson.

23 Wigfield, A., Eccles, J. S., Schiefele, U., Roeser, R. W., & Davis-Kean, P. (2006). *Development of achievement motivation*. John Wiley & Sons, Inc.

Learning Outcomes

24 Bloom, B. S., Engelhart, M. D., Furst, E. J., Hill, W. H., & Krathwohl, D. R. (1956). *Handbook I: cognitive domain*. New York: David McKay.

25 Krathwohl, D. R. (2002). A revision of Bloom's taxonomy: An overview. *Theory into practice*, 41(4), 212-218.

Scholarship of Teaching & Learning

26 Boyer, E. L. (1990). *Scholarship reconsidered: Priorities of the professoriate*. Princeton University Press.

27 Biémar, S., Daele, A., Malengrez, D., & Oger, L. (2015). Le « Scholarship of Teaching and Learning » (SoTL). Proposition d'un cadre pour l'accompagnement des enseignants par les conseillers pédagogiques, *Revue internationale de pédagogie de l'enseignement supérieur*, 31-2. http://journals.openedition.org/ripes/966

28 Lison, C., Bédard, D., Beaucher, C., & Trudelle, D. (2014). De l'innovation à un modèle de dynamique innovationnelle en enseignement supérieur, *Revue internationale de pédagogie de l'enseignement supérieur*, 30-1. http://journals.openedition.org/ripes/771

Teaching and Learning Theories

29 Bourgeois, E. & Chapelle, G. (2011) *Apprendre et faire apprendre*, PUF.

30 Chalvin, D. (2012) *Histoire des courants pédagogiques: Tome 1, Encyclopédie des pédagogies pour adultes*, ESF.

31 Cooper, P. A. (1993). Paradigm Shifts in Designed Instruction: From Behaviorism to Cognitivism to Constructivism. *Educational Technology*, 33(5), 12–19. http://www.jstor.org/stable/44428049

32 De Corte, E. (2010). *Les conceptions de l'apprentissage au fil des temps. Dans OCDE, Comment apprend-on ? La recherche au service de la pratique*. Éditions OCDE. http://dx.doi.org/10.1787/9789264086944-fr; https://doi.org/10.1787/9789264086944-fr

33 Ertmer, P. A., & Newby, T. J. (2013). Behaviorism, cognitivism, constructivism: Comparing critical features from an instructional design perspective. *Performance improvement quarterly*, 26(2), 43-71.

34 Hativa, N. (2001). *Teaching for effective learning in higher education*. Springer Science & Business Media.

35 Jarvis, P., Holford, J., & Griffin, C. (2003). *The Theory and Practice of Learning*, Routledge.

36 Livre Blanc : La place des 5 grandes théories de l'apprentissage dans la formation. (2019, September 12). *Sydologie*. https://sydologie.com/2019/09/la-place-des-5-grandes-theories-de-lapprentissage-dans-la-formation/

37 Woolfolk, A. (2018). *Educational Psychology* (14th Edition), Pearson.

Impressum

Acknowledgments	We would like to thank all the people who read and commented on draft versions of this book. We are most grateful for the support given by the University of Lausanne and the College of Humanities at the Swiss Federal Institute of Technology in Lausanne (EPFL), which helped bring this project to life. We would also like to acknowledge Yves Pigneur and Alexandre Osterwalder who provided the inspiration for our approach. And finally, we would like to express our gratitude to the participants in the training workshops held at the Teacher Support Center (CSE) at the University of Lausanne, whose questions and comments allowed us to develop our approach.
Graphic design and illustrations	Julian Bader
Translation	Jo Nicoud-Garden
Fonts	Sang bleu: Swiss Typefaces VTD Handmade: Julian Bader

English edition 2024

Épistémé is an imprint of the Presses polytechniques et universitaires romandes
ISBN 978-2-88915-629-0, print version
ISBN 978-2-8323-2262-8, ebook (pdf), doi.org/10.55430/8024VA01

The digital version of the book was funded by the Gold Open Access Fund at the University of Lausanne.
The translation was made possible with a grant from the University of Lausanne Publication Fund.

UNIL | Université de Lausanne

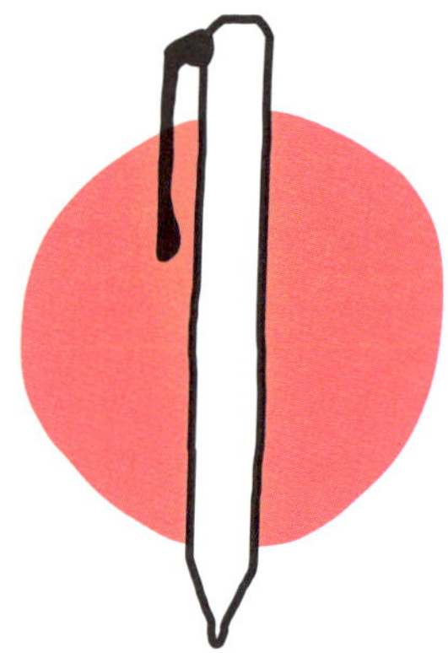

Visit our website for more digital tools

Join our Course Design community
to keep up to date with recent developments
and contribute to the canvas and its uses

designpedagogique.info